Frank O'Hara

STANDING STILL AND WALKING IN NEW YORK

Edited by Donald Allen

Grey Fox Press
Bolinas, California

Cover photograph of Larry Rivers and Frank O'Hara by Renée Sabatello Neu.

The Edward Lucie-Smith interview is published with his permission and by courtesy of the Humanities Research Center, The University of Texas at Austin.

Grateful acknowledgment is made to the following who first published many of these works: American Composers Alliance, *Art News*, Brandeis University, Canyon Books, Columbia Records, *Evergreen Review*, *Folder*, Grove Press, *It Is*, The Kulchur Foundation, *Poetry*, The Poets Press, *Studio International*, *Village Voice*, *Vogue* and *Yugen*.

Gregory Corso's "In the Tunnel-Bone of Cambridge" is reprinted from *The Vestal Lady on Brattle* by permission of the publisher, City Lights Books, San Francisco.

Frank O'Hara's Introduction to *Dancers Buildings and People in the Streets* by Edwin Denby, copyright © 1965, is reprinted by permission of the publisher, Horizon Press, New York.

The following are reprinted by permission of Alfred A. Knopf, Inc. from *The Collected Poems of Frank O'Hara*, edited by Donald Allen: "About Zhivago and His Poems," "Statement for *The New American Poetry*," "Personism: A Manifesto," "Statement for Paterson Society," "Notes on *Second Avenue*," and "Larry Rivers: A Memoir." Copyright © 1959, 1960, 1961, 1971 by Maureen Granville-Smith, Administratrix of the Estate of Frank O'Hara.

O'Hara, Frank.
   Standing still and walking in New York.

   I. Title.
PS3529.H28S7   811'.5'4   74-75455
ISBN 0-912516-13-5
ISBN 0-912516-12-7 pbk.

Grey Fox Press books are distributed by Book People, 2940 Seventh Street, Berkeley, California 94710.

CONTENTS

"Standing still and walking in New York" comes, of course, from Frank O'Hara's "Ode on Causality." It was to have been the title of an essay describing his life in the city he planned to write for a special New York City issue of *Evergreen Review* I proposed to edit back in 1959. In the end neither essay nor issue was to materialize.

Yet he did describe his life in several ways—in his poems, and in these essays, prefaces, reviews and in the interview. They show very clearly his stance, his concerns enthusiasms loyalties annoyances and distrusts; they give us the ambiance, mode, rhythms of his metropolitan life.

Some of these pieces have been retrieved from Frank O'Hara's papers and are published here for the first time. "Design etc." appears to be notes for a talk given at The Club in 1952. "Notes on *Second Avenue*," "Gregory Corso," and "A Personal Preface" were perhaps written for magazines or books; *Roma* was turned down by the editor it was sent to, "Statement for Paterson Society" was never sent to Ellie Dorfman, and "Apollinaire's Pornographic Novels" seems not to have been completed.

When the George Braziller editors decided to limit their *Art Chronicles* to a selection of O'Hara's art criticism, I felt the omitted essays must also be included in this volume, in order to get all of O'Hara back into print.

I am particularly grateful to Edward Lucie-Smith for checking the transcription of his interview, and to Mrs. Mary M. Hirth and David Farmer of the Academic Center Library, the University of Texas, for supplying us with a copy of the tape and giving us permission to publish this unique interview. I am also much indebted to Bill Berkson and Ted Berrigan, Norman Bluhm, Morton Feldman and Ben Weber, Alison Lurie and Bradley Phillips, Valerie Estes and Joe Bacon for assistance in editing this volume.

D. A.

An Interview
with
Frank O'Hara

EDWARD LUCIE-SMITH:
AN INTERVIEW WITH FRANK O'HARA

[This informal interview was taped during two sessions in O'Hara's 791 Broadway flat in October 1965. A much abbreviated version was published in *Studio International*, September 1966. Ed.]

SESSION ONE

LUCIE-SMITH: What I wanted to ask you about, first of all, was this business of the literary link and the painting link with you. It seems as though much more in New York there is this link between poetry and painting.

O'HARA: Well, it's partly I suppose because of the French influence, in a way, on American painting. You know the Apollinaire, cubism, and all that sort of thing. And then the other thing is that for a certain number of people whom Barbara Rose recently referred to in *Art Forum* . . .

L-S: Yes, I saw that.

O'H: as unemployed poets who worked for art magazines and wrote art criticism. When we all arrived in New York or emerged as poets in the mid 50s or late 50s, painters were the only ones who were interested in any kind of experimental poetry and the general literary scene was not. Oh, we were published in certain magazines and so on, but nobody was really very enthusiastic except the painters.

L-S: And why do you think that was? Because the painters were more committed to an idea of experiment than the literary were?

O'H: Yeah, exactly.

L-S: And how would you say that this has affected you? You ought to talk specifically on New York poets.

O'H: Well, partly because I think the *example* of certain of the abstract expressionists in particular and then later other artists in New York and in Europe gave me the feeling that one should work harder and should really try to do something other than just polish whatever talent one had been recognized for, that one should go further.

L-S: Do you see yourself as a kind of collaborator with painters? I know you've made poems . . .

O'H: No, only. Not at all. Only in one specific instance when Larry

Rivers and I actually did physically collaborate on some lithographs called *Stones*. Which were called *Stones* because we both did work on them. I learned how to write backwards, for instance. We did not use any transfers. We worked on the stones together. He did not work on the stone if I wasn't there and I didn't work on the stone if he wasn't there to see what I was doing. Sometimes we would discuss the placement of an image which would leave me enough room to write the text, or I would say where I wanted the text and then he would decorate the rest of the stone. But that's the only time I think that I've really collaborated. I've done other things where some — well Grace Hartigan has used some of my poems in painting. Or I have made pages of words for Michael Goldberg which he then completed, but I delivered them in those cases, and then they went on and did what they wanted. I didn't have any say about what they would do with them. I was very pleased with the results. I think the Rivers thing is the only thing I really did collaborate on, that I consider to be a collaboration.

L-S: Isn't this something rather unusual in a museum official? Museum officials are usually thought of in Europe as codifiers of art, a final court of appeals, but not as the participators.

O'H: Well, it's a little more complicated than that because after all Jean Cassou is a poet, isn't he? And in America it's very hard to codify the art as it emerges anyway, so that your participation is really your interest in a sort of emotional way which leads you perhaps to understand a little bit better than the general public at the time the work is appearing. And then you're either right or wrong later.

L-S: Which way do you think things are going in America? You've been very much, obviously, identified with Rivers, partly because you collaborated with him, and partly because you were painted by him.

O'H: You mean do I think they're going towards Rivers or away?

L-S: Well, that's as good a question as any to start off with, at least it's concrete.

O'H: I don't feel particularly identified with Rivers. I mean we're friends, but then I'm very very close friends with other painters whose work I also admire so I don't, you know — the fact that Larry did paint me at a certain time or that we collaborated on this set of lithographs — I don't think . . . I think he's a very individual artist and therefore it would be very difficult to say that any particular trend was exemplified in his work. One thing that he did manage to do, which was quite

significant I think, was to admire and be influenced by abstract expres-
sionism as a younger person, a younger man than the heroes of it, and
find a way to keep working in a valid, interesting way.

L-S: As a figurative artist then?

O'H: Well, not even particularly figurative. I think, for instance, that the
influence of Gorky on Rivers is extremely strong. As is, in some
periods, the influence of Léger, for example. And it is not very often
recognized in American criticism, because the transition into pop art
has been so fast in the public attention, that where Rivers would be
discussed would be as the forerunner of pop art instead of the really
interesting thing, which is the way he used the influence of de Kooning,
of Léger, of Gorky, and even in many cases of Kandinsky in his work,
though it may be related to images of Camel packs, of lions walking
through the streets of, you know, the language books where the parts
of the body are spelled out, and stuff like that.

L-S: Well, let's make a quick jump here to something which Henry
Geldzahler said to me — he talked quite a lot about a tradition, of
working in a tradition. If I kind of throw this word "tradition" at
you . . .

O'H: Yes. Well, who talked about it, Henry? Or . . .

L-S: Yes, Henry.

O'H: On behalf of what artist?

L-S: On behalf of op artists, mostly. Like Poons and so on.

O'H: Poons?

L-S: But what I want to get hold of is essentially your reaction to this
idea of tradition. You've talked, for example, of Rivers almost building
on the theories of other artists.

O'H: Yeah, like every artist does. I mean you don't really think that Bill
de Kooning is lying when he says that he loves Poussin or Ingres? Or,
if Motherwell says he loves Delacroix, you can certainly see it. For
instance, it was an absolute revelation to me, I think, in a certain light
in the Louvre when you see *The Raft* of Gericault and *The Massacre at
Chios* that the purples are practically black and there are an awful lot
of them. They're great, slashing hunks of purple. You know at another
time of day, let's say if you go at ten o'clock in the morning, it all looks
as if it's really quite something that Meissonier might be very pleased to
have done and would have been in a particularly turbulent mood when
he did. But if you see them at another time of day, in the late afternoon,
they're not totally unrelated, say, to something like *The Elegies to the*

Spanish Republic or to the late abstractions of de Kooning.

L-S: Well what excites you most in modern American art? What are the
qualities you find yourself responding to?

O'H: Well, they're all individual qualities. I would really just have to
name a lot of artists. I don't find that one year I'm excited by abstract
expressionism, the next year by pop art, the next year by op art, and
then this coming year by spatial sculpture, or something. You know.
It all is in the same environment which I live in.

L-S: What I'm talking about is this: That in Europe, styles are apt to
arise, or in England, styles are apt to arise and then be packaged. In
New York it must be very different because . . .

O'H: Oh yes, because you know the work before the style has even been
established.

L-S: Yes.

O'H: You see.

L-S: And therefore . . . What I'm looking for particularly is your sense
of the connections between things which are usually held to be very
different in England.

O'H: Well, I wonder if, for instance in Europe, one would really . . .
You know everything gets so codified here, too. That is, certain people
seem to think of cubism as if it suddenly sprang from the head of Zeus
and it wasn't called Minerva. Therefore, there were no fauves, there
were just the cubists. There were no synchronists. You know, nothing
else was happening at the same time. And then the relations between
the things changed too. The cubist Légers of the smokestacks, you
know, the chimneys, for instance, are just as closely related to fauve
painting as they are to cubism. They're not totally flat. They don't
show the volumes from the other side. They are involved with color.
The City of Léger in the Philadelphia Museum: it's a cubist work cer-
tainly, but it has fauve color. Delaunay — now where do you put Delau-
nay in that sort of thing? So that it's very difficult for me to imagine
New York as not having, say, Larry Rivers and Larry Poons in it at the
same time, along with Al Held, John Chamberlain, Anuskiewicz. They
all exist, you know, in one's milieu so we see them, we see them from
week to week. You go from one thing to another. It's hard to pick out
any mainstream thing, except for the individual artists whom one admires.

L-S: Yes, but let's pick up two questions here. One of them is: do you
think American art has separate characteristics which make it American?

O'H: That's a horrible question.

L-S: I know but it's difficult to put it any other way.

O'H: I know. Does one think that Tapiès' paintings are that way because he's Spanish?

L-S: No, that's not quite it. Even more than that. Do you think of Tapiès as a kind of provincial in relationship to New York?

O'H: Oh no. Not at all. No, I think the work of Tapiès in New York, as in France or in Spain or in Italy, is an absolute fact of contemporary art. See, the general mistake, I think, is in thinking of these things in terms of nationalities. There *is* modern art.

L-S: But you don't detect a specifically American flavor, not even an American tradition?

O'H: I think Pollock was absolutely right when he said, and I don't remember it exactly, but he said there is no such thing as American painting or any other kind of painting. There is good painting. Or something like that, he said it during the text of the movie that was made of him, in his own voice. And I can't remember it exactly and I don't have it here. But I do think that's a very important point. That there is good painting and there's bad painting and there's indifferent painting and there's superficial painting and there's frivolous painting. This also goes for sculpture, poetry and anything else we are all involved in. You know. And I don't think that the Americans or anybody else has any option, it depends on the individual artist.

L-S: What do you think about the idea of the New York "Underground" which has been such a journalistic issue recently?

O'H: Well, what do you mean?

L-S: "Underground" movies for example. Warhol. This kind of thing. I mean the kind of activity which is connected with the art world of New York without being specifically painting.

O'H: Oh, happenings and so on.

L-S: Yes.

O'H: Well, it's an acknowledgment . . . I think actually that in many cases it's an acknowledgment of the best work of a lot of other people. And not to be misunderstood or to have a misunderstanding. If so much really marvelous work hadn't been done in the twentieth century by artists of a great many nationalities, there would be no . . . Wait, let's put it — I was going to say there would be no necessity for Andy Warhol to decide to devote himself to films. I'll put it more positively — he would not feel that it was OK for him to devote himself to films. But if he does so, then it must mean that he as an artist assumes that

a great deal of pictorial and sculptural imagery has been dealt with ad-
equately *in* painting and sculpture but *not* in films. I think most artists
take the, most responsible artists, and Andy certainly is one — no mat-
ter what set of rumors go around about him — improve the medium
they choose. In times of desuetude you find Rembrandt laboring over
etchings because there are no great etchings after Seghers in that period,
and Rembrandt is taking a responsible attitude towards the medium.

L-S: You see one of the things which I talked about with Henry Geld-
zahler was the idea of the underground versus the idea of the avant-
garde, in the sense of the need for the embattled vanguard and . . .

O'H: Embattled? That's interesting. There is no underground and there
is certainly no embattlement. Andy Warhol gets more publicity than
any other single living American artist right this minute. And if that's
supposed to be underground, when you cannot even open a fashion
section of the *Herald Tribune* without seeing his name at least once
a week, then that's not being underground. So that I think that's a
lot of nonsense. And there's a whole Cinemateque on Lafayette
Street to show those movies. They have their own . . . Even most
Hollywood producers don't have their own showcase in New York.
They have to farm it out to the Albee-Fox and so on. They're depend-
ent on managers, business managers, to do it. I don't think that's
being very underground. I don't mean that I'm saying that it isn't a
good thing; I think it's terrific. But it is not being underground; that's
a lot of romantic nonsense.

L-S: I think it is romantic nonsense myself. But I think that it puts ex-
tremist art in a new position. That you have for the first time a de-
liberately extremist art with a ready-made audience, with an acceptive
audience.

O'H: Yes, I do too.

L-S: And what difference do you think this makes?

O'H: I think it makes it, it puts it back . . . I would think that if I were,
if I had been . . . Ah, that's too silly a thing to say but I'll say it any-
way. If you were an Athenian, let's say, and you saw, if you went to
the studio and you saw the eyeballs being painted and the nipples
being painted and so on, I should think it would be just as sensational
as if you were invited to a private showing of *Flaming Creatures* of
Jack Smith.

L-S: Yeah.

O'H: You know it's the same thing because it is part of your culture and it's coming on with . . . It is not attacking us really in a certain way, and there's no reason to attack a culture that will allow it to happen, and even foster the impulse — and create it. Which is a *change,* you see, from the general idea of, that all avant-garde art has to be attacking the bourgeoisie, and the bourgeoisie has now been so completely absorbed by the rest of society that it can't even have its prejudices any more.

L-S: Do you feel that the avant-garde no longer exists in a state of detachment or isolation?

O'H: No, the avant-garde always exists in the state of idea. That is, the avant-garde has been made up, I think, completely, and all through history, with people who are *bored* by other people's ideas.

L-S: Yes.

O'H: Now, you do not have to have the Russian Revolution or the French Revolution or the Civil Rights Movement in order to get irritated by other people's ideas. All you have to do is be one individual who is tired of looking at something that looks like something else.

L-S: Yeah.

O'H: If you're a painter, then you make it look like something that nobody saw before, if you can, if you can think it up.

L-S: This is a kind of dynamic of impatience which you're proposing.

O'H: Yes, and boredom. Western civilization, however, has really put a, laid an awful load on that thing because so many things have already been done. What would you do that would be different and not boring?

L-S: You think it's important to be new then?

O'H: No, I think it's very important not to be bored though.

L-S: Let's switch to, a moment to . . .

O'H: No, I think that — to make it clear — I think that if de Kooning says that, then what he really is interested in is Poussin; that's his way of not being bored with Kandinsky, or *by* Kandinsky. You see, when all the world is looking at Kandinsky, he suddenly says I think Ingres and Poussin are the real things to look at. Now it may only work for two years, but that doesn't matter in the life of the artist as long as it energizes him to produce more works — that are beautiful.

L-S: Let's switch a moment to, inevitably — since I live in England and work in England's terms — I'm always very interested by the way the English scene reflects America. Are there things which attract you, excite you, in English art at the moment?

O'H: Oh, yes.

L-S: What kind of things? Which artists?

O'H: Oh well, I think there are a lot of injustices going on, personally.
      One is that the pop art thing in America has been almost universally
      assumed to be American, which it isn't. Since, if I remember cor-
      rectly, as early as about 1952 or 3, pop art, as we know it today and
      as it was indicated, was already being done in England.

L-S: Yes.

O'H: The British public has had the most enthusiastic response to the
      most important American artists, more than in America.

L-S: And you feel that?

O'H: Yeah. Though I think that in many cases, in the case of Pollock,
      of — certainly of Pollock, Rothko and Rauschenberg and Jasper
      Johns — not Jasper so much because he did have a good response
      here — it was after the London exhibitions that Americans snapped
      to and said, boy we've really got something here now, we'd better
      start studying it and thinking about it and feeling something about
      it. And I'm not talking about what happened later when certain
      British artists were influenced by it. Now the same thing of course
      happens in the reverse sense with Francis Bacon's first show in New
      York, which absolutely bowled everybody over here. And he is a
      magnificent artist certainly. But they weren't even paying that much
      attention to *Pollock*! And I don't mean to raise my voice that high
      when I say that, but it is sort of funny because, in the meanwhile,
      Pollock was in fact at his death, he was at the end of his career. So I
      think that's one thing that cultures can do mutually back and forth,
      is to appreciate the elements which are too close to you and you don't
      really look at.

L-S: Do you come to London?

O'H: No. I've never been there at all.

L-S: You've never been?

O'H: No.

L-S: Well, what excites you of what comes over?

O'H: Well, my total experience really is, you know, flush with loan ex-
      hibitions and things like that. And then I was enormously impressed
      by the Paris Biennale which had Philip King, David Hockney and
      others. It was certainly the best national representation in that inter-
      national exhibition. I was enormously enthusiastic about that. And
      then, of course, Moore's undeniable. I don't personally feel very

inspired by, say Butler or Hepworth. They're not very distinctive are they?

L-S: No, I won't concede that . . .

O'H: And then of course there's always that thing of the Whistler-Turner combination in the consciousness of all Americans. That Whistler did live in London, and Turner did do those paintings.

L-S: So Turner, you feel, is almost, by kind of adoption, an American artist?

O'H: No. But I think . . . No. No more than, say, the late Monet is. Everybody knows that he's a British artist. And that's not the point. You don't adopt him. He adopts you, if you're lucky enough.

L-S: Yes, well there's a real sense isn't there in which Turner's a kind of Whitman of painting, at least he's the equivalent . . .

O'H: Oh, he's a more . . . No more specifically . . . Not so much that way. Not in the emotive way. It's more that – I would imagine that say, that – apart from influence – I would find it more difficult, much more difficult, to understand an artist like Philip Guston if I didn't know Turner's work. And I don't think that Guston is particularly influenced by Turner. It's just one of those things that happen in time and in history.

L-S: Is it that your feeling toward Turner illuminates Guston for you?

O'H: Yeah. I don't know . . . I never even asked Guston whether he was interested in Turner. I can't imagine he wouldn't be. But, you know, I don't know that it was a specific influence; just that when *I* think about it, it does seem to help me to understand what Guston is doing.

L-S: One thing I'd just like to check up on is a bit of fact, and that is your actual career in the New York art world. When did you go to work for the Modern?

O'H: I first worked there in 1951 and 2 because they needed some extra people because they were having an Henri Matisse retrospective and it was so mobbed that they didn't have a big enough staff. And then I left to work for *Art News* as a reviewer, and then I went back in 1955 . . . This is really quite funny since my general tendency has been to work on American shows ever since, except for Spanish exhibitions. So I was asked to come back to work on the "De David à Toulouse-Lautrec" exhibition which was made up of masterpieces from American collections. And then I've stayed there ever since, more or less.

L-S: In the exhibitions department?

O'H: Yeah. In the foreign exhibitions.

L-S: But you had established yourself as a poet, to some extent, before
      you ever went to the museum, hadn't you?

O'H: I wouldn't say "established," no. I don't know as I'm established
      now.

L-S: Well, in that case, perhaps we can gradually glide into our other
      subject for a moment. And that is . . . I am interested in the process
      of establishment, not . . . I don't mean . . .

O'H: You mean getting established?

L-S: I'm interested in the methods by which poets reach their audiences
      and the kind of poems they come to them in. You have published a
      book with City Lights, *Lunch Poems*, and you've published another
      book which I have, which is called *Second Avenue*. Which has the
      Larry Rivers' cover on. And these were in a sense the product of a New
      York experience, I feel very much. That they are about . . .

O'H: Yeah. Well the thing is that I'm very influenced by Reverdy, for
      example, or by Whitman to a certain extent. But very much the French
      poets because I think that one thing the American poets make too
      much of after Whitman and which was ruined to a great degree — I
      mean it could have kept it but it didn't — because of the New Criticism
      and certain rather stupid ideas about how, about what is the comport-
      ment in diction that you adopt. Whitman embarrasses an awful lot of
      people, probably still. And he certainly did during the 30s and 40s
      when Hart Crane was probably the only person who wasn't embarrassed
      by him. It seems to me that in the 30s and 40s there were an awful lot
      of dicta laid down by everybody about what was good and what was
      bad without any consideration of what was valuable.

L-S: Why do you think that the valuable . . .

O'H: And I mean like Eliot saying you're not supposed to read Milton,
      and so on. You know. Which is ridiculous.

L-S: Which angle do you see yourself from? You know the usual dichot-
      omy which is put up for one now, arriving as one does all innocent in
      America, is the dichotomy between the raw and the cooked or between
      the academic and the Black Mountain, or between Lowell and Olson.
      These are the kinds . . .

O'H: Yeah.

L-S: How do you see yourself? I hate to *force* these kind of polarities on
      you. It's unfair. But I think it would be useful to begin by asking how
      you feel yourself to be placed in relation to them.

O'H: Actually I don't really see what my relation is to them one way or the other except that we all live at the same time. I think that Olson is — a great spirit. I don't think that he is willing to be as delicate as his sensibility may be emotionally and he's extremely conscious of the Pound heritage and of saying the important utterance, which one cannot always summon up and indeed is not particularly desirable most of the time. And I think Lowell has, on the other hand, a confessional manner which [lets him] get away with things that are really just plain bad but you're supposed to be interested because he's supposed to be so upset.

L-S: [*Laughs.*]

O'H: And I don't think that anyone has to get themselves to go and watch lovers in a parking lot necking in order to write a poem, and I don't see why it's admirable if they feel guilty about it. They should feel guilty. Why are they snooping? What's so wonderful about a Peeping Tom? And then if you liken them to skunks putting their noses into garbage pails, you've just done something perfectly revolting. No matter what the metrics are. And the metrics aren't all that unusual. Every other person in any university in the United States could put that thing into metrics. So I don't really associate very much with it. I would *rather* be the sort of poet who would do, you know, the great thing of, you know the story about Max Jacob leaning out his window when Picasso is passing by the Bateau-Lavoir and Picasso calls up and says, "Max, come out." And he says, "I won't." He says, "Why won't you?" And he says, "Because I'm in search of a style." And Picasso walks down the hill and, as Max Jacob pulls his head back, says, "There is no style." That is the sort of thing that is, you know, like living and interesting.

L-S: Well what you're advocating then is something which is detached, self-contained and self-respecting, and therefore free.

O'H: Well, it's hard to respect yourself, but I would like to be free. I mean I don't know what there is to respect, but let's not get into that. [*Laughs.*]

L-S: No, what I'm talking about is that your poems seem to have a kind of urban wariness. Wariness or weariness. Not a cynicism but a kind of self-containment. And what you've just said about Lowell is in fact very characteristic, it seems to me, of your own verse.

O'H: Yeah. I really dislike dishonesty [more] than bad lines, in a certain way. Because I don't think there is such a thing as a bad line if it's true. The metrics make it, you know they get there themselves. If you really are being honest about something, then the metrics just devour them.

L-S: Well, what's the criterion of truth in poetry?

O'H: Where you don't find that someone is making themselves more
      elegant, more stupid, more appealing, more affectionate or more
      sincere than the words will allow them to be. Now I know I do it my-
      self, you know. I can see it when I reread some of my poems that I
      went overboard and that the words are showing quite clearly to any-
      one who's bothered to look at them closely enough: that it's bullshit,
      you know. And that's what I don't like. I would like to take it out of
      my work, and I don't like it in other people's work. If I could get it
      out, you know. By then it's too late . . .

L-S: But do you think that this kind of element of the avoidance of
      bullshit also enters into the painting which you like?

O'H: Yeah. I imagine that where I got the idea was probably from the
      abstract expressionists who have consistently tried to avoid that. As
      compared, let's say, to the American cubists, and I would say Stuart
      Davis, for instance, of certain masterpieces of his — and I do admire
      him as a painter — they're confections.

L-S: Yeah.

O'H: There is no, there are very few Clyfford Stills that are confections.
      And whether you like them or don't like them, there they are and
      there they stand and that's that.

L-S: Oddly enough for me they do have a kind of confectionary look. I
      was looking at a whole room of them in the Albright . . .

O'H: Yes. No. I don't think they do any more than — I saw that room in the
      Albright, and I don't think they do any more than autumn does. And
      I don't mean he's a great natural phenomenon either. I mean there's
      something sort of hokey about autumn leaves turning red and brown
      and all that too and yellow, but I think he had the really genuine thing
      there.

L-S: I think what you're talking about, aren't you, is — thank god we're
      not on wireless so I can construct the words — but is the kind of, what
      you're talking about quite a lot of the time is the process of becoming.
      Of things becoming, of yourself becoming, of paintings becoming. Do
      you understand what I mean?

O'H: Uh uh. Yeah, I certainly am.

L-S: And this seems to me a characteristically American thing. I think
      that if you talk to Americans of all kind of literary complexions, and
      indeed of all complexions in the art world, that this is the common,
      that you feel that this is the common characteristic almost.

O'H: Well no, because I was talking in a negative way about what I don't
like, you see. I was saying what I think is the impediment to that,
which is not to imply that certain things haven't already become it.
I don't think that there's anything more to — I think, for instance,
that other people have said other things. Franz Kline, for instance,
and Pollock when they died didn't leave anything undone except
what they would have invented. They had become it. They did do it.
Anymore than Whitman should have written another book, i.e. maybe
he should have, it would have been marvelous if he had, but he didn't
have to, though.

L-S: Well, there was already an achievement created which was suffi-
cient?

O'H: Yeah. So that it isn't just a process of becoming because I don't
think that American art has to become anything now. It can add to
itself. Well, you know, apart from the natural ambitions of anybody
who is talented. But there are certain masterpieces of American art,
as there are of British art and Egyptian art and so on, which have al-
ready, they're already doing their own work. They exist and there they
are.

L-S: And you don't feel this inclination to denounce, for example, the
American art world, which many Europeans feel when they come to
New York, because the dynamic is a financial dynamic, quite apart
from everything else, and a dynamic of publicity?

O'H: Oh no, it's no more financial in character than anyplace else, and
Budapest is just as financial. I don't think that has anything to do
with anything. Enthusiasm for art, after all, is always involved with
any number of interesting attitudes. Everybody wants to have a jewel.

L-S: You think that this is a kind of ownership thing as well, this en-
thusiasm?

O'H: Of course . . . Now that's silly to even talk about because the
basic human motive is acquisitive.

L-S: That's a terribly American thing to say. [*Laughs.*]

O'H: Well, it's not American. What about Windsor Castle? What about
the Elgin Marbles?

L-S: Well, one of the things which appear in, it seems to me to appear
more and more in Europe, and I think in a more concealed and veiled
way in America, is that art is very much becoming . . . It's not be-
coming something you own, but it's becoming — an event which you
go to experience in a museum. Museums are becoming more and more

theatres of a certain kind of emotion.

O'H: The only reason why that's happening, I think, is that probably because Americans have more money recently than they used to have and they are able to cross larger areas of space, which Europeans never even had to bother doing, so that it is possible for an American to go to Ghent. Whereas it was always possible for a Londoner to go to Ghent. And naturally the more you travel and you see master-pieces — and they are usually in the museums and cathedrals . . .

L-S: Are you not more moved by being in a Catholic church than you are moved by being in a museum?

O'H: But the excitement in America, you see, is that finally there is, there are, some people who have enough money, who are able to travel to places which Europeans were always able to travel to. They could even take a third-class train and do it, where we couldn't. So they are used to their experiences in the Louvre now. They're used to the Uffizi. They're used to the Tivoli Gardens and so on. And that is a happening for an American. Whether it's a happening which they respond to ancestrally in the sense of what their forebears told them about these marvelous things or whether it's something that they just love because it's an event that they arrange themselves. It is not — only recently have Americans even bothered, for instance, to trot off to Philadelphia to see the museum on a Saturday. It's perfectly avail-able.

L-S: An hour and a half on the train.

O'H: Yeah. And people didn't do it until very recently. And it's somehow that that has become an event. And I think that the happenings, for instance, are very closely related to reconstruction of aesthetic events which you see in museums in Europe, especially, because they're more exotic which you travel further to enjoy.

L-S: Well, but a happening is a kind of removal, in fact.

O'H: Happening is just like a little play. There's nothing mysterious about it at all. They never were anything more than that and the whole mys-tique of them is absolute nonsense. They're improvised plays. Every-body's done them, and done them, and you've done them yourself as a child. They're always — that was their great charm, that they just happened because somebody wanted to do them and they wanted to invite a few people who usually came to the gallery, or whom you *liked* to come and see them. It always was. The Jim Dine ones, the Oldenburg ones, the Red Grooms ones — they were always done in a

certain manner of "I'm going to do this delightful thing, I *think,* and I
hope you'll come and think it's delightful."

L-S: Have you taken part in happenings?

O'H: No, I never did.

L-S: You've only been a witness?

O'H: Yeah. But I did get that . . . I took part in them in the sense that
I got that tone of it. If Red Grooms decides that he's going to paint
his face white, get into some old-fashioned underwear, have a drain
dragged across the stage, if a tree is going to fall over in a Jim Dine,
and if something in an Oldenburg is going to collapse — that is for your
fun. It's supposed to remind you that art is fun and that we're all child-
ren and that it's marvelous. That's *all* they meant by them. It is *not*
existential, you know, or propaganda for any movement.

SESSION TWO

O'H: Where were we?

L-S: I think we were talking about sincerity in poetry and you were
saying something to the effect that you would rather be true than
conventionally good. A bad line which was truthful was likely to be
a better line than a conventionally good line.

O'H: Yes, that's right. Yeah. Because it seemed to me that the metrical,
that the measure let us say, if you want to talk about it in Olson's
poems or Ezra Pound's, comes from the breath of the person just as
a stroke of paint comes from the wrist and hand and arm and shoulder
and all that of the painter. So therefore the point is really more to
establish one's own measure and breath in poetry, I think, than — this
sounds wildly ambitious since I don't think I've done it but I think
that great poets do do it — rather than fitting your ideas into an estab-
lished order, syllabically and phonetically and so on.

L-S: Well this is, to switch back to painting for a moment, this is some-
thing which is true of quite a lot of American painting: that it's trying
to establish its own gesture apart from the established order. This is a
parallel case, wouldn't you think?

O'H: Yes, and that's what I meant about being — that I think certain
poets have been very much inspired by American painting. You know,
not in the sense of subject matter, or anything like that, but in the am-
bition to be that, to be the work yourself, and therefore accomplish it.

L-S: I'd like to switch this slightly on to something I always, to my in-
terest, have great difficulty explaining in America. That it seems to
me that compared to Europeans, Americans have a very much more
rudimentary sense of themselves as — not as individuals — but as
parts of the social whole, and that the American sense of cohesiveness
is much less, that a great deal of the American effort goes into being
an individual and to placing oneself as an individual, but not into
thinking . . . not sort of thinking of oneself as a part of something.

O'H: Yes, it's true. And in the sense that Europeans are very often
surprised at, say, if you have an American artist and you are to, oh,
give a party for him. Then you would have a very wide range of people
who are not, who may or may not know each other. In fact the person
that you give the party for would be the only cohesive element which
will link them all together. For instance, it's always very interesting
that, say, it is not surprising at a party at Bill de Kooning's studio to
meet Harold Rosenberg. And it's also not surprising to meet an atomic
physicist, who will turn out to be a very good, old friend of de
Kooning's. You know. And you can see it. That it's perfectly obvious
that they've had endless talks together. They understand each other
perfectly well. Whereas, I think, in European circles the social area is
much more definitely established. There aren't these strange buckaroos
whose interests you wonder about, and this sort of thing. Now what
does this businessman care about abstract expressionism?

L-S: Well, there's another thing where it shows, isn't there, and there's
much less done, I think, in the realm of *travaux d'équipe* in America.
That such collaborations as there are, like happenings, are improvised.
Immediate collaborations. They're not deliberate things of the kind
that you've had in France and also to some extent in Germany
recently.

O'H: They are made . . . I'm thinking particularly of, let's say, the
happening which had a text by Kenneth Koch and a construction
by Jean Tingueley and a collaboration by Bob Rauschenberg and Niki
de St. Phalle and Merce Cunningham. All of them joined in this effort,
which ended up being called either the construction or the destruction
of Boston — I forget which way it went, since there was so much going
on — and they were all battling till the very moment the curtain went
up about what direction it was going to take. And I don't mean in an
unpleasant way, but they were — you know, it really was a collabora-
tion in the sense that nobody had, absolutely, made themselves the key

figure in it. They were still arguing about what would happen when Jean would go on and build the wall, what would happen, what was going to be said, Kenneth was still writing. You know, the whole thing was really very lively and exciting. And it wasn't . . . in that sense it was not at all like a play although it had a script. It really was a happening.

L-S: To just sort of turn for a moment to more kinds recently of sensational events, I understand that there was . . . we talked about Andy Warhol last night . . . I understand that it was riotous, his opening, down in Philadelphia.

O'H: Oh yes, I just heard about it, though I didn't go to it. Henry Geldzahler was there. Well, there was quite a great riot at his opening where he had all the boxes. You know, the Brillo boxes and the others . . .

L-S: Why do you think that he has acquired this quality of, I think, manner is the right word, this kind of magic?

O'H: Because he's . . . I think it's because Andy has a tantalizing imagination. He knows *exactly what not* to do and what to do and how diffidently to do it for the right moment in the cultural history of, you know, of a certain city. Whether . . . Now, for instance, I think that here we have not seen − or the public has not seen − as many of the serious paintings as you have in London and Paris. They were not shown. The civil rights pictures weren't shown. The Kennedy things were shown in a, you know, in this very minor way. The flowers were, for instance, the last show. The Brillo boxes. It's something . . . I don't know how it happened. I mean, I don't know why, in a way. So that you find that, in my experience, Europeans take him much more seriously in relation to his subject matter as a painter. And the American audience takes him more seriously as a provocateur, almost − you know − like a descendant of Marcel Duchamp, but not as a social critic in his work.

L-S: Do you think that he is a genuine descendant of Marcel Duchamp?

O'H: Well, I don't know. Well, actually, he is awfully interesting because he makes everybody look again at painting or try to think of what it is: what is it really? what do you want? why do you not want it and so on. In that sense he is a marvelous provocateur. The other thing, of course, that I think that's missing in the general American evaluation of Andy's work is exemplified, let's say, by my − I went to Boston recently and saw the full mounting of the picture of Mrs.

Kennedy. You know, the one with the silk screens.

L-S: Yeah.

O'H: Now, that is as big as that Goldberg over there, in its full scale. It was never shown in New York full scale. And it's absolutely moving and beautiful. Not sarcastic, and it's not some sort of stunt. It really is complete compelling work when shown in the way he wanted it to be shown. When it's as big as it's supposed to be and there are that many images of her and the color somehow works from image to image. And I think that he — you know, just as one knows that Duchamp's serious — I think Andy is a terribly serious artist rather than an agent to make everything lively, which he sometimes is taken for in the United States. The European evaluation of him is much more exact.

L-S: Well, he certainly seems to have this strong streak of feeling for tragic subjects. The Marilyns are tragic pictures too.

O'H: Yeah. And also his whole idea of making icons, for instance, which is presumably one of the . . . You know, maybe they're not real icons, but there's some sort of almost religious element in them — in his motivation to make them the way they are.

L-S: Do you feel that this is a sort of — a part of — the way that things are going in American art. Really I asked you about Warhol because it seems for some reason quite a good stepping off ground to talk about your feelings about art, in general, in the United States.

O'H: Well I think the most . . . Oddly enough, it seems to me that the most original work is being done right now — except for the people who are already acknowledged as original creators — in sculpture, as I think it probably is true in England. Some of the sculptors like George Sugarman and Ronald Bladen are doing, you know, really *very* original and interesting things. And, at the same time, people whose work has been perhaps a little bit neglected — or at least sort of in the background of rather elite taste — are becoming much more assimilable. Say Barnett Newman and the sculptor and architect Tony Smith. And Tony Smith, for instance, whose ideas have been influencing people for several years, but no one really looked at his work, you know. And now, because of these younger people, it is possible to find people who are interested enough to investigate Tony Smith's work and his ideas in a much more tangible way. Before it seemed to be like theory, same thing of course is true of [Buckminster] Fuller and the geodesic dome and so on. Suddenly it has become a reality.

It's not just some wonderful idea someone has, you know.

L-S: But don't you think that one of the characteristics of American painting, as of American poetry, has been this business of the foreground and the background. I told you I'd just been to see Zukofsky, and it seems that in a sense Zukofsky has existed on the second plane. That the real importance of Zukofsky, up till very recently, has been the influence he has exercised over the people who were in the public eye.

O'H: Yes. He's like the Buckminster Fuller or the Tony Smith of that . . . you know, of the generation he's in. Now, Allen Ginsberg, for instance, *ten* years ago was *trying* to make people pay attention to Louis Zukofsky, and nobody would. And it's partly because he was overshadowed by Ezra Pound so completely, in a way. And Pound is such a great genius that he really was associated more as a follower, you see, than as an originator. And then it's only recently . . . That goes for Olson too. It's only recently that young poets, who, like the young sculptors I was talking about, have made people see what there was there, or is there I should say, by their own work and by the intensity of their interest.

L-S: Have you ever hesitated between being a painter and being a writer?

O'H: No, I can't say that I have.

L-S: Did you work as a painter ever?

O'H: Just fooling around. I mean I've just fiddled around — as a matter of fact mostly through my friendships. If I was in some studio waiting for them to finish working, I might do some little thing, you know. But I never really did it seriously because I guess I don't have the . . . It seems to me that painting and sculpure take so much concentration over such a period of time that I'm not so sure I can do it. Whereas one *can* write relatively fast. And also I've gotten very discouraged when I've tried to paint, and the harder I've tried the more muddy it gets. I don't really know how to resolve my own ideas in the medium and get anything that satisfies me really.

L-S: This element of speed is important in writing . . .

O'H: Yes, I don't believe in reworking — too much. And what really makes me happy is when something just falls into place as if it were a conversation or something. As for instance, well to take Keats for example, it doesn't much matter if he did work very hard because it seems as if he didn't. And, you know Yeats had that marvelous remark about if all the stitching and restitching does not seem to be the effort of the moment

it is all in vain, or something like that. And I think that's, of course,
also the quality that marvelous painting and sculpture has. It looks
like it took about three seconds, in a way. A Matisse, for instance,
seems to be simply the result of a lot of talent, thoughts, and every-
thing, but that the actual execution took practically no time at all.

L-S: Well, it's hard to believe the comment that Larry's picture of you
took such a very long time to paint.

O'H: Oh, well, that's nice . . . that's very flattering for Larry. It cer-
tainly did take months of posing.

L-S: But it looks so spontaneous in handling.

O'H: Yes. I think . . . well, partly because it was the . . . You know,
of course the whole thing about the Géricault inspiring it, and I
think what Larry was trying to do was to keep it from being academic.
But at the same time getting into the ring with Géricault . . .

L-S: Well, let's talk a bit about the way things are going. We've talked
about, you know, the way things are.

O'H: Let's say about to become. That's asking an awful lot cause it's
all guesswork. Well, what do you mean?

L-S: Well, what do you see coming up in American poetry first of all?

O'H: In American poetry?

L-S: Yeah.

O'H: Uh. Well, there are a number of interesting things. For instance
there's a poet named Tony Towle who has this marvelous diction
which is out of Wallace Stevens, I think, but just as I said — you
know — that say John Ashbery and Kenneth Koch and I, I think,
were quite influenced by abstract expressionism's powers and per-
sonality, Tony Towle seems to be quite influenced by the ideas
around Andy Warhol. With this beauty of diction coming from
Wallace Stevens which is really quite an alarming and interesting
style to get to know.

L-S: What has he published in?

O'H: I would guess in very little magazines. I mean he's been in *Art
and Literature* and in *Locus Solus,* I believe. And I think he was
published in . . . yeah, he was published in *Poetry* Chicago, but
in general he's published in magazines like *C* of Ted Berrigan and . . .

L-S: He hasn't published a little book yet?

O'H: No, not yet. No. Then there are other poets like Frank Lima and
Jim Brodey. Frank Lima's work seems to be more or less out of
William Carlos Williams and *direct* frontal assault on your own ex-

periences in an autobiographical sense. Brodey seems to be mainly influenced by the French surrealists in the way that Americans have been, but in a more direct way. It's, you know, the sort of tumultuous outpouring of images which then get themselves together into being a poem, somehow. But you do have the excitement of seeing whether you're really going to get it to be a poem or not. You know, or is it just going to be a . . . But of course with the influence of Levertov and Creeley you have another element which is making *control* practically the subject matter of the poem. That is your *control* of the language, your *control* of the experiences and your *control* of your thought.

L-S: Yes, somebody once said to me . . . that Creeley was so busy telling you what he was going to write and how he was going to write it that he never got around to writing it.

O'H: It is amazing that Creeley puts as many vowels in as Levertov, and the amazing thing is that where they've pared down the diction so that the experience presumably will come through as strongly as possible, it's the experience of their paring it down that comes through more strongly and not the experience that is the subject, you know. In some cases, not in all.

L-S: But it looks to me, you see, coming from outside and England, that there were two traditions in American poetry going, both of them having their roots somewhere in Stevens but having other roots elsewhere in each case.

O'H: Yeah.

L-S: But Stevens seems to be the point of branching — and that one of these traditions, which is the one which is best known in England, the Anne Sexton, Robert Lowell and the sort of Lowell followers like Seidel and so on, and that this tradition seems to have been broken off short; and that suddenly it is the vital tradition, it's the tradition which comes through William Carlos Williams and Olson and Creeley and Levertov.

O'H: Yeah, and I think it's partly because it's so, that is you think that the . . . well the thing is that there are certain people in America — and I am not one of them — who feel that, let's say, the two greatest works on American literature are the D. H. Lawrence book [*Studies in Classic American Literature*] and the William Carlos Williams' book *In the American Grain.* That already gives you an orientation which we never had, and it's easier in a way to appreciate the value of those books if you're *terribly* interested in European literature too, because

somehow the experience, you know, makes everything clear. But if
you can make some distinction, then you can really see what is up
and what isn't. Now the absorption of Lowell in the *imitations* of
Pasternak, of Rilke and so on is domesticating in a certain way. That
is, it's domesticating those poets into really pretty much New York-
like, not even American-like. Whereas the attraction that, say,
Ginsberg feels for Pasternak and Mayakovsky, or the attraction that
Kenneth Koch feels for Tzara, Breton and Eluard . . .

L-S: He also feels an attraction for Pasternak and that kind of thing
as well?

O'H: Yeah, and so therefore he is not domesticating those poets into
American life. He sees that an American has to join that other life,
and that's quite a different . . . And it really is quite a signal of a
different kind of talent but also a different kind of mind, a different
kind of ability, an ability to empathize outside. But somehow it has
made a more American and more vivid style, I think, for Koch, let's
say, than the imitations did for Lowell. It seems to me that the im-
itations are all part of the corpus of Lowell's work more than they
are the poets that are being imitated.

L-S: Do you read the young English poets? Are you interested? I always
find that there's an odd kind of gap across . . .

O'H: Yes, there is. There's a big gap I think in my thinking about English
poetry, although for instance I admire very much Tomlinson and Thom
Gunn. We all, I think, got stuck on Auden and MacNeice in a way. That
is, they're just so good that it's absolutely swamped . . . They really
captured us and, as a matter of fact — like last year, for instance — I
was giving a few readings. And finally I was so tired of reading my own
work and everything, I read all Auden's things and some MacNeice and,
let's see, one poem of Wallace Stevens. But I found that when I read
The Orators, which I read the whole of the book because it's been out
of print for some time and Auden has repudiated some of the poems and
everything, and as a work, however, it goes streaming along like the most
marvelous thing imaginable. And I think it was also the most satisfying
reading I ever gave of anything. You know, much better than my own
work.

L-S: Yes, Auden, in fact, is marvelous. I've never thought of this before,
but *The Orators* does seem to look like a certain kind of American . . .

O'H: Yeah, well it's had such influence here, you see, it's washed back
onto *The Orators* and given it a marvelous tone. Even the structure of

it, as a book, has had an enormous influence on American writing. I don't believe for one minute, for instance, that the airmen business in it has failed to influence Terry Southern, who immediately dreamed up *Strangelove*. You know, the sheer flippancy and sarcasm and *accurate* satire is very important.

L-S: And yet Denise Levertov said to me, for example, that she felt no contact with Auden's later work.

O'H: Well, the thing is that — the poem about art . . . This was . . . when I did the reading, for instance, it was before MacNeice had died. However, it didn't surprise me at all that Auden could write a great poem about the death of a friend. As a matter of fact, he's such a great master that it's very moving — even to have him in operation in the same time that you live is thrilling. And besides, of course, it depends on what you really love. Now, for instance, in "In Praise of Limestone" he's going along and then he says, "Green places inviting you to sit." That's worth a whole career to have a line like that. A career anyplace. Whether it's in an editorial in the *Times* or wherever it may be.

L-S: Are you attracted by Auden's sort of deliberately artificial side, this kind of conscious virtuosity?

O'H: Oh I'm attracted to it because it's something that one should know. But what I'm really attracted to, I guess, more, is a certain dashing, Byronic . . . You're sort of galloping into the midst of a subject and just learning about you, you know. You're not afraid to think about anything and you're not afraid of being stupid and you're not afraid of being sentimental. You just sort of gallop right in and deal with it.

L-S: Like the "Letter to Lord Byron," for example.

O'H: Yeah. right.

L-S: This is all of course very different from England, however, where we still have this business of poets being one down from critics. This doesn't seem to happen at the moment in America.

O'H: Well, that's because you're talking to poets. No, there is a big . . . One of the most infuriating things in American literary life — which gets us back, as a matter of fact, to what I was talking about, you know, the fact that painters have been such a marvelous audience for younger poets — is that in the rest of the literary life in America the work, the original work, the novel, the poem, the play, whatever it may be, is supposed, you know, is really tacitly assumed to be the raw material for a wonderful piece of criticism, in the tradition of R.P. Blackmur, who writes a more beautiful essay than all of Henry James's novels put together. His interpretation of *Anna Karenina* is better than the novel. There's a, you know — so that you really think that Robert Frost and Lowell and all those people are dumping their raw material into the mind of this critic who will then place it in history. And, of course, by the way, themselves. And it is a tacit assumption on the parts of, let's say, of the *New York Review of Books* that the books are — it's wonderful that they're published because that gives them a chance to bring out their paper and then they can really tell people that they don't have to read the books at all, what they really ought to do is think about their opinion about the books.

L-S: Well, since such was the milieu I began in as a writer, I'm terribly conscious about the extent to which poems in England are checked by critics to see if they respond to the reigning formula. The critic is only willing to be excited by that which is already covenanted for.

O'H: Yeah, that may be true in dealing with poetry. It's also partly the fault, I think, of the generation of British poets after Auden and MacNeice.

L-S: Which generation do you mean, the Dylan Thomas generation or the Larkin generation?

O'H: I mean the Larkin, Amis and so on generation. Because it seems to me that the minute you try to establish — and I don't know why they want to do it in a way and in another way I sort of assume that I do know — the new bourgeoisie sensibility, then you are getting poetry into a situation where there can be regular formulae that have to be observed. I think what William Carlos Williams was always trying to do was to keep us away from that. That's why he did all those diatribes against the sonnet.

L-S: Your phone!

O'H: I know it. Can you stop this record?

Notes & Essays

AUTOBIOGRAPHICAL FRAGMENTS

[1]
Hats! that's what I think of when I think of Baltimore in 1926 (truly a
strange year to be born!), because my father (unless I came from the
gypsies) was working in a hat-and-shoe store, or haberdashery, and this
is my only pre-natal connection. Post-natal, I suppose, is my affinity
for magnolias and tulip trees, but who doesn't have that? therein doesn't
lie the significance of being born in Baltimore. But there was something,
if I could only remember it, because it made me unhappy all through my
childhood in New England, and it wasn't till I got to Key West and the
Pacific islands that I realized what had been bothering me.

Almost all data relating to my birth adds up to 6, which is curious, and
I am an ardent horoscope reader, favoring particularly Constella, though I
dislike her changing my zodiacal designation from Cancer to Moon Child-
ren. Be that as it may, the most hopeful day of my life, that day when she
advised me to meet some influential people in the Ritz Hotel in Boston, I
had not enough money to go to the Ritz, which I immediately noticed
had something to do with the number 6 in a crap game. I soon gave up
such ambitions, and am now only relatively harassed by worldly concerns.

Nevertheless I am aware that I am now six years older than Keats was
when he died and four years younger than Byron when in the the same
situation.

But how odd it is to think of my childhood in New England, the alien-
grass section of the USA. I read somewhere that it's supposed to be a
matriarchy there, but all I remember from my early childhood is men,
with a few worried, whining and submissive women trailing after in my
[. . .]   [1960]

[2] *
My earliest political memory is of being dragged by my father into a bar-
bershop in a small New England inn for a haircut. I hated the smell of the
place (which I later came to associate with funeral parlors) and what I felt
was the hypocritical considerateness of the barbers (which I later came to

*This piece is an excerpt from a long autobiographical fiction tentatively
called *A Short Unhappy Life*. FOH.

associate with the anterooms of funeral parlors), but I loved a huge brilliants-encrusted metallic blue and gold and white hanging calendar depicting a foaming glass of beer, the date 1933 and the legend HAPPY DAYS ARE HERE AGAIN. I was seven, and it is perhaps because of this experience that, no matter how much I may admire or dislike a pop art work, I can hardly ever find its image shocking or particularly unusual in motivation.

How happy I was then! politically speaking. Most of the adults I overheard in this mainly agricultural town were optimistic about Roosevelt, I was crazy about his campaign song, and Labor Unions were something I hoped to find out about later, along with the Foreign Legion. There were a lot of Republican families around, of course, and not only had I been vindicated by history in my thought that there was something a little too piggish about Landon's face, but I had also won a lot of bets off the friends who had written Anti-Roosevelt slogans on our windows that Hallowe'en. The blind lady who lived next door had a cat, which she called to chow about six times a day: it's name was NIRA and only many years later did I think with fondness of the old lady's fondness for what I was not understanding in the Saturday afternoon newsreels. But I still do. And in a way she is a touching example of the American conception of political purity: it should be blind and fond, and quickly domesticate its ideal — and once domesticated the ideal should be overfed.

I was sent against my will to Catholic schools, but fortunately I also began at the age of seven to study music. A lot of my aversions to Catholicism dumped themselves into my musical enthusiasms, and in a sense a lot of my vague political thinking is still felt musically. (I can't believe the Russians are all bad, but I can see how the Germans might be. Hitler could have easily been inspired by Brahms as by Wagner, the system is equally intrepid. As my good friend Arthur Gold once said when we were discussing how to play one of the Brahms intermezzi, "When you get it right it sounds gorgeous. Like shit. Completely brown.")

I had rather summarily deduced that my whole family were liars and, since our "community" consisted of a by and large very mixed national descendency it couldn't be that they were Irish liars, they must be Catholic liars. Had I been a French child I probably would have simply become an anticleric; as it was, I blamed almost everything onto the Catholic Church, which they all talked about in the most revoltingly smarmy way (a priest once later said, trying to win me over, that I had been overparochialized!). I left the Truth to Music.

At any rate we are now approaching 1940 at a leisurely pace, and my next political memory was that of revulsion at having been made to pray for Franco's success during the Spanish Civil War when I was in grade school and didn't know which side was which. By the time I read *For Whom the Bell Tolls* (which also introduced me to the most attractive aspect of John Donne) this made me furious, and still irritates me in a metaphysical way.

[3]
"So you think you're going to be a great pianist," my father said to me in 1943, "say, like Rachmaninoff?"

"Yep," I said, "and a composer too."

"Hmmmm," my father said. My mother was eating an apple.

"What's the matter, don't you think I can?"

"Well, I think it's more difficult than you do, apparently."

My mother put down her apple and sighed. "I may as well tell you, Russel," she said, "that he's already told me about his great plans. I think it's depressing. The other day when I was in Worcester I stopped in at a bookshop and read some of Mozart's letters. Really, that poor man had *such* a miserable life! I'd just die if I thought he was going to be a composer. They have such terrible lives, I can't begin to tell you."

"So what?" I said. "And anyway, all of them didn't. Just a few."

"Now wait a minute," my father said, glad to have the opportunity to be more permissive than my mother, for once. "If we don't let him, he'll always think we stopped him. And it isn't so very much money, after all."

My mother sighed again. "I'm not going to argue with *both* of you. But when it all began, remember, we just wanted him to have some general culture. I didn't want him to become an addict!"

I pulled my trump. "Then why have you made me practice every day since I was seven years old?"

"I don't know," my mother said. "I can honestly say I don't know."

"Maybe she just liked to have you around the house," my father said.

"Really! I liked to hear him play, that's all."

"You see?" I said joyfully. "So will everyone else!"

"All right," my father said. "You can't say in afterlife that we stood in the way. Go ahead. Learn the hard way."

"Okay," I said.

And so I began studying piano at the New England Conservatory. It was a very funny life. I lived in Grafton, took a ride or a bus into Worcester every day to high school, and on Saturdays took a bus and a train to Boston to study piano. On Sundays, I stayed in my room and listened to the Sunday symphony programs.

[4]
CAHIERS: It was a very depressing week, and not just because of the rain, which it wasn't particularly often anyway. Bleak and full of nasty little surprises. There you are in the Cedar minding your own business when someone walks up to you and says. "I know who you are. What do you think you're up to, anyway?" and walks away. Then someone in the Remo says, "How come you've gotten to be such a name-dropper? You didn't used to have to do that to bring off a poem. Mike Goldberg! come on, now." Meanwhile, back in the Cedar I walk in and someone says, "Soandso just got a job on some magazine or other, I hope it isn't an art magazine because she agrees with me that when you write about art it's awful." Now this would be all very well if I were an injustice collector, but since I can never decide whether it's justice or not, it's not so cute. At the same time at least they think about you, but is this the famous Saloon Society made famous by the *Village Voice*?

[5]
Through habits of thought, feeling and judgment, a poet looks at things a little more peculiarly, if not entirely more peculiarly, than others. For one thing, the habit of esthetic rather than moral values tends to absorb one's attention and one's "slant." This may even amount to a prejudice, and at the very least is a strong bias.

DESIGN ETC.*

*1. A plan, formed in the mind, of something to be done or produced; a
mental project or scheme in which means to an end are laid down; as a
design for a revolution; also, a preliminary intellectual conception, as of
a poem or an argument.*

*2. Purposive planning as revealed in, or inferred from, the adaptation of
means to an end or the relation of parts to a whole . . .*

Let us assume that a fairly good definition of design, for our purposes,
not for all purposes, may be arrived at through distinguishing between
form and design. I would say that design as it relates to and exists in Poetry,
is the exterior aspect as opposed to the interior structure which we call
form. Form may be completely mysterious to the reader, though nonethe-
less real in its existence and causality; design must be apparent, it *is* that
which is apparent to the eye and ear. This is not to say that the design of
a poem is a negligible quality. As I hope to show, it is a very important
part of the work and indeed contributes a great deal toward establishing
the identity of the poet as well as of the poem.

To take the simplest aspect of design in poetry, and the most external,
there is the look or format, which strikes both ear and eye. This element
is very clearly and easily apprehended. When you think of e.e. cummings,
in whose work design is very important, you think immediately of his identi-
fying characteristics, and what you are thinking of is design: the small case
letters in his name, small case letters throughout the poems, elaborate use
of parenthesis and typographical arrangements. Reading the poems aloud,
the ear hears the line by line and stanza by stanza arrangement, if not the
distinction between capital and small letters. In the latter connnection, it
is interesting to note how many contemporary poets emphasize the visual
rather than spoken organization of the poem.

Apollinaire, in his *Calligrammes,* designs the format of the poem so that
it visually resembles his subject: in *"Il Pleut "* the lines fall down the page
like drops of rain, elsewhere he will make the words about smoking take the
shape of a pipe, and there is a poem about France and Germany which takes
the form of the Eiffel Tower. These are very obvious examples of design. . . .

The long, involved and rather grandiose lines of Whitman, each almost a
paragraph, must be read and heard in a noble Homeric tone; the short line

*These appear to be notes for a talk at The Club in 1952. Ed.

33

for love lyrics and meditations (say Byron's "So we'll go no more aroving")
must be read slowly, and the poet governs the speed by making the eye
drop and by closing off each individual line with rhyme. This more sub-
tle use of design in poetry, unlike the calligram, is very generally observ-
able in varying degrees and tends to disappear in the total poem, diffusing
itself into the formal aspects. But insofar as we feel the "personality" of
the poet in the poem, as opposed to what the poem says literally, design
is present. Where design is weak, oddly enough, the form is usually strong
and may even be the reason why the design is weak. How many boring
poems there are whose form is like cast iron; the poem not only is pre-
vented from breathing, but the poet is so stifled by the formal restrictions
he has imposed on his work that no individual design can possibly appear.
Let me read you two poems, one to show design; one to show form with-
out what I am choosing to call the quality of design. (W.C.W. and some-
one else.)

The distinction I am trying to make between form and design is per-
haps arbitrary, but while they are both undeniably similar they are not
necessarily aspects of the same thing. George Herbert's devotional poems,
for instance, often have shapes (a chalice, a diamond) and that is their
design; the form however is the traditional rhymed metaphysical medita-
tion, with the favorite metaphysical rhetorical characteristics including
the farfetched images called "conceits"; in Herbert's case the design is
very clear, the form very obscure, for the form cannot be clearer than
the meaning of the poem.

I do not mean to convey the impression that design is always a good
thing or that when I use the word I am only indicating pleasant character-
istics. In Herbert's case, for instance, one may be put off by the naïveté
of shaping a religious lyric of passionate intensity like a chalice. Certainly
it shows peculiar taste. A more admirable use of such out-and-out typo-
graphical tricks is in Apollinaire, who usually indulges this whimsy only
when he is writing a light, witty poem. There it appears clear, amusing
and indeed could not be otherwise: you have a distinct feeling that some-
thing is wrong when you see one of these poems printed in traditional
stanzas, which is of course the ultimate test of design.

For some other instances of remarkable and strong design, I would
cite at random: Ezra Pound, Marianne Moore, Charles Olson (whose
theory of projective verse, among other things, recommends the use of
the typewriter as an instrument, not just as a recorder of thought), Wal-
lace Stevens, W.H. Auden. Of Stevens, W.C.W. has said that he did not

invent forms, but used those available to him, and this is true of the element of design in his work: it is clear Anglo-French, delicate, like Mallarmé, as is also that of T.S. Eliot.

So far I seem to have emphasized the visual and typographical appearance of design. It also works beneath the surface of the poem and still does not slip into the category of form, because it is not part of the same structure emphasis that form is. How does it work? Design guides, it seems to me, the meaning through the formal rapids of the poem's requirements and restrictions past Scylla and Charybdis into open water. If we do have a menacing pair ready to reach out and murder this meaning, Scylla would be the poet's associations with the forms he is using, associations with the use of that form on previous occasions by himself, and the stunning triumphs of others with that form, so in a way he is virtually arming the form against himself and not too infrequently the form will take the poem right away from him and run off into the distance with the speed of half-thoughts, turgid emotions, secondhand insights, and all the rest, including a pat ending. The other monster, the Charybdis, is the poet's passion for poetry and his own ideas: this too will tend to run away with the poem and after it has happened a few times, the poet feels that his emotions are more important than any poem, that indeed they, not words, *are* the poem. After this has happened a few times, the poet is bored with poetry, can only write when he is emotionally hopped-up or is self-excited. Neither of these ogres is very easy to avoid, but design is the point where the poet can hold his ground in the impasse between formal smothering and emotional spilling over. In this sense design need not be apparent typographically, it is a clearheaded, poetry-respecting objectivity, without which the most sublime and inspired love lyrics or hate-chants would just be muddy rantings. As the poem is being written, air comes in, and light, the form is loosened here and there, remarks join the perhaps too consistently felt images, a rhyme becomes assonant instead of regular, or avoided all together for variety and point, etc. All these things help the poem to mean only what it itself means, become its own poem, so to speak, not the typical poem of a self-pitying or infatuated writer. For a dramatization of this little scene and a few asides on bad poets, let me read you a little of Kenneth Koch's poem "Fresh Air." (Auden and Millay)

In recent poetry what one may call properties of design have often been introduced as corrective of formal habits, asking that the bases of such elements as placement, metrical regularity and measure which had

been felt more as deadening than adventurous. So we had, after the French
and German Dadaists, such innovations as José Garcia Villa's comma
poems (which are actually traditional lyrics with commas between each
word or letter) and the phonetic analyses of Edith Sitwell (the fruity O,
the piquant short i, etc.), and the occasionally sarcastic typography of
e.e. cummings, which are satires on traditional poetic forms and senti-
ments.

NOTES ON *SECOND AVENUE*

These notes which I'm attaching to the excerpts sometimes indicate, be-
cause you requested it, a more detailed identification of the subject mat-
ter (in some cases just a last name) than I wanted in the poem itself because
it is beside the poem's point in most cases; elsewhere the remarks are ex-
planatory of what I now feel my *attitude* was toward the material, not
explanatory of the meaning which I don't think can be paraphrased (or at
least I hope it can't).

This thoroughness whose traditions have become so reflective,
your distinction is merely a quill at the bottom of the sea
tracing forever the fabulous alarms of the mute
so that in the limpid tosses of your violet dinginess
a pus appears and lingers like a groan from the collar
of a reproachful tree whose needles are tired of howling.

To put it very gently, I have a feeling that the philosophical reduction
of reality to a dealable-with system so distorts life that one's "reward" for
this endeavor (a minor one, at that) is illness both from inside and outside.
There are several scenes in the poem with characters, for instance
(briefly) a flier in his plane over the ocean:

"Arabella" was the word he muttered that moment
when lightning had smelled sweet over the zoo of the waves
while he played on and on and on and the women grew hysterical.

a little Western story, beginning:

The Western mountain ranges were sneaking along "Who
taps wires and why?" like a pack of dogies and is there much
tapping under the desert moon? Does it look magical
or realistic, that landing? And the riverboat put in there,
keeps putting in, with all the slaves' golden teeth and arms,
self-conscious without their weapons, Joe LeSueur,
the handsome Captain who smuggles Paris perfumes, tied up
at the arroyo . . .

37

(Joe LeSueur is a friend of mine, a novelist not published yet)

a newspaper clipping report of Bunny Lang's trip in the Caribbean:

"Nous avons eu lundi soir, le grand plaisir de rencontrer
à l'Hôtel Oloffson où elle est descendue, la charmante
Mlle. Anne R. Lang, actrice du Théâtre Dramatique de Cambridge . . ."

a true description of not being able to continue this poem and meeting
Kenneth Koch for a sandwich while waiting for the poem to start again:

Candidly. The past, the sensations of the past. Now!
in cuneiform, of umbrella satrap square-carts with hotdogs
and onions of red syrup blended, of sand bejewelling the prepuce
in tank suits, of Majestic Camera Stores and Schuster's,
of Kenneth in an abandoned storeway on Sunday cutting ever more
insinuating lobotomies of a yet-to-be-more-yielding world
of ears . . .
                    (he was continuing to write his long poem as he waited)

a talk with a sculptor (Larry Rivers, who also sculpts) about a piece in
progress:

Your feet are more beautiful than your father's, I think,
does that upset you? admire, I admire youth above age, yes,
in the infancy of the race when we were very upset we wrote
"O toe!" and it took months to "get" those feet. Render. Pent.
Now more features of our days have become popular, the nose
broken, the head bald, the body beautiful, Marilyn Monroe.
Can one's lips be "more" or "less" sensual? . . .

a description of a poetry critic and teacher: (tirade?)

                    A chicken walked by with tail
reared, looking very personal, pecking and dribbling, wattles.
You suddenly got an idea of what black and white poetry
was like, you grinning Simian fart, poseur among idiots
and dilettantes and pederasts. When the chips are in,
yours will spell out in a wealth of dominoes, YOU, and you'll

be stuck with it, hell to anybody else, drowning in lead,
like your brain, of which the French poets wrote, "O fat-assed
configurations and volutions of ribbed sand which the sea
never reaches!" Memories of home, which is an island, of course,
and historical, of course, and full of ass, of course. Yes,
may you . . .

a description of Grace Hartigan painting:

and when the pressure asphixiates and inflames, Grace destroys
the whirling faces in their dissonant gaiety where it's anxious,
lifted nasally to the heavens which is a carrousel grinning
and spasmodically obliterated with loaves of greasy white paint
and this becomes like love to her, is what I desire
and what you, to be able to throw something away without yawning
"Oh Leaves of Grass! o Sylvette! oh Basket Weavers' Conference!"
and thus make good our promise to destroy something but not us.

Oh, I forgot to excerpt something else, a little description of a de Kooning
WOMAN which I'd seen recently at his studio:

You remained for me a green Buick of sighs, o Gladstone!
and your wife Trina, how like a yellow pillow on a sill
in the many-windowed dusk where the air is compartmented!
her red lips of Hollywood, soft as a Titian and as tender,
her gray face which refrains from thrusting aside the mane
of your languorous black smells, the hand crushed by her chin,
and that slumberland of dark cutaneous lines which reels
under the burden of her many-darkly-hued corpulence of linen
and satin bushes, is like a lone rose with the sky behind it.
A yellow rose. Valentine's Day . . .

Actually, I am rather inaccurate about the above, since it is a woman I
saw leaning out a window on Second Avenue with her arms on a pillow,
but the way it's done is influenced by de K's woman (whom he thinks of,
he once said, as "living" on 14th St.).

I don't know if this method is of any interest in taking little pieces of
it. You see how it makes it seem very jumbled, while actually everything
in it either happened to me or I felt happening (saw, imagined) on Second

Avenue. Where Mayakovsky and de Kooning come in, is that they both
have done works as big as cities where the life in the work is autonomous
(not about actual city life) and yet similar: Mayakovsky: "Lenin," "Eiffel
Tower," "150,000,000," etc.; de Kooning: *Asheville, Excavation, Ganse-
voort Street,* etc.

As I look this over, it seems quite a batty way to give information about
the poem, but the verbal elements are not too interesting to discuss although
they are intended consciously to keep the surface of the poem high and dry,
not wet, reflective and self-conscious. Perhaps the obscurity comes in here,
in the relationship between the surface and the meaning, but I like it that
way since the one is the other (you have to use words) and I hope the poem
to *be* the subject, not just about it.

                              Sincerely,

NATURE AND NEW PAINTING

When one speaks of nature's role in painting, it always becomes a star one, for the very word *"nature"* has prestige in our prejudiced ears. And what does "nature" mean in relation to "painting"? It depends on the historical period. There is natural painting, called such because the talent of the painter seems to encounter no obstacles, to appear before our eyes as characteristically as his handwriting. But there are also paintings of and about nature, paintings which are permeated by the feeling of nature and which represent the perfected observation of nature's detailed structures and even selflessly proclaim principles of nature which the artist has perceived.

Cézanne perceived the structure of natural forms as well as their look and feel and this is not "extra," not apart from the esthetic value of the work. Do I think that, amassing a fortune of dirt, rocks and trees, following a Cézanne word for word, I could put together a hill which would not fall down? Well, great painting does make one feel like God. Among other things, art gives us ability, knowledge, even when it tells us what we do *not* know, what has *not* happened. Cézanne perceived the meaning of objective reality in terms of its construction as a philosopher perceives the clarity of a moral situation. Mondrian did the same thing in his early work. When, later, his perceptions began to operate on a more general site, his paintings stated these perceptions without generalizing — they remained art; he approached profundity and grandeur, for his perceptions seemed to embrace all the structures of nature. Like Cézanne, he had seen into the heart of nature. This is not to grade his achievement, but if his late work is a limit it is one of knowledge more than of style.

To think that late Mondrian is "painting about painting" is a grievous error; great art, except in baroque periods, is seldom about art, though frequently its insights are so compelling and so pervasive they can be applied to art as well as to their subject; often we find their moral application acceptable. Yet when Keats wrote, "Beauty is truth, truth beauty," — it is a grievous error to think that he was writing about writing poetry. His insight into the structure of human sensibility (if this seems tautological, one may remark on Rilke's insight into that of animals and angels) is no more merely against the ugliness of lying than Mondrian is against paintings which do not affirm the horizontal and vertical (in his work). That is too narrow an application. From the impressionists through the cubists to the present, art has been involved with nature.

There is a kind of painting, too, which *looks* to be about nature but is lacking in perceptions of it. Here the painter utilizes his visual experience for subject matter, but his experience is the subject, nature is not, and therefore the structure we observe is that of his experience rather than of what he has experienced. Certain impressionist pictures seem lightweight perhaps because they only offer us anecdotes about nature; the real subject is not nature, but portraying nature, and while it may be very beautiful it is less grand to observe the structure of artistic effort as a metaphor for the structure of nature itself. To place such an impressionist painting next a late Gorky would be to see the difference very clearly.

Modern life has expanded our conception of nature and along with it nature's role in our lives and our art — a woman stepping on a bus may afford a greater insight into nature than the hills outside Rome, for nature has not stood still since Shelley's day. In past times there was nature and there was human nature; because of the ferocity of modern life, man and nature have become one. A scientist can be an earthquake. A poet can be a plague. In the abstractions of Willem de Kooning and in his female figures, we perceive structures of classical severity: the implacable identifications of man with nature. This is not symbolized. It is painted. In a manner of speaking, this artist's great *Excavation*[1] shows us what we do to the earth just as his *Woman*[2] shows us what we do to women. So deep an insight into the structure of man's identification with nature and the play of forces which it involves cannot be discussed in terms of passion or of plasticity, terms which are only useful in discussing the talent and skill of the painter, not the achievement of the paintings themselves.

The poet, Edwin Denby, penetrates the meaning of our response to a work of art as well as the achievement of the work itself. And perhaps the latter is truly secondary, for the achievement of a work of art changes but our response to it is a precise instant in the accumulation of its meaning and benefits from clarification. We do not respond often, really, and when we do, it is as if a flashbulb went off. Mr. Denby's criticism helps us to gain and to govern these otherwise capricious revelations. Ballet is illumined by his intuition; our best contemporary art critics are preoccupied with assessing, surveying, tallying and rating — with history and with the history of painters, less with the achievements of the paintings themselves and our response to them. The last two decades have been filled with baroque art-to-art cant: like the rumors that swept through Europe after Columbus' voyages, there has been a great vulgarization and falsification of the discoveries of early 20th century masters. At the same time there have been other voyages, given impetus by the eternally powerful examples of Cézanne — it was not just the Indies after all.

Had it not been for the adventurous spirit of American abstract-expressionism we should have been given over to a cult of mechanics, of know-how, of push-and-pull spatial organization which, as a means of formal knowledge, is essential perhaps, but which cannot be confused with creation, that word we use for a perception which is staggeringly original to us. Painting exists in time as precariously as a voyage or a ballet and it is dangerous not to respond — more dangerous to respond to rumors. When we consider painting and time the work of Franz Kline stands forth as heroic. Like a juggler, he forces the weight of the world to his fingertips and then, for brutal passages of black paint and white paint, gravity ceases; of the most gigantic energies a particular poise is demanded and won.

What is this poise? It is the passionate attention of natural forces (in painting everything is animate) to the innermost will of the artist, and in this respect Kline is most tender. He speaks to the volcano in a whisper. Or, if you prefer, he removes the thorn from the lion's foot. To perceive the natural forces which his paintings hold in abeyance is a unique experience of our time and makes his position in our society as meticulously extreme as that of Ingres in his, compounded as it is of insight into and resistance toward those forces of nature which we find ourselves as men identifying with, however fearfully.

It is this atmosphere, I think, which has led many young painters to a closer perusal of nature and while one cannot isolate the quality of this atmosphere with the term "perception" that term figures clearly in their work. Turning away from styles whose perceptions and knowledge are not their own occasion, these painters seek their own perceptions and in doing so have turned, voluntarily or involuntarily, to nature, their way made clearer by the Gorkys and de Koonings which they admire but do not emulate. Is this Naturalism? Not in the sense of "realistic method" certainly, though perhaps in the sense of "adherence to nature, indifference to conventions."

Two years ago in a talk at the Hansa Gallery, Clement Greenberg declared that abstraction was the major mode of expression in our time, that any other mode was necessarily minor; this was straight observation from the point of view of historical criticism. But a year later James Fitzsimmons, writing in *Arts and Architecture,* remarked that some of the young painters had lost heart and abandoned abstract-expressionism in cowardly fashion to

return to representational work. It is against just such an implied protocol
that abstract-expressionism has always taken up a strong position, whether
at the Metropolitan Museum or the Artists Club. Among the painters who
rebelled against this notion while still incorporating elements of the for-
mal structure of the preferred style are Robert De Niro, Elaine de Kooning
and Grace Hartigan and, as with any rebellion, the retained elements work
for these artists in an unusually provocative way. Mr. De Niro, whose early
expressionism had French color and an earnest, elegant clarity in its light
and in its feeling towards the subject illuminating the quality of the forms
as they appear to the air around them (giving *Woman with a Parasol,*[3] for
instance, a repose which is perceived in the figure though the painting it-
self is active and dashing), moved in later paintings towards a greater for-
mality achieved by imposing upon the iconography slashing strokes and
surrounding blacks (from Hofmann, I think, as much as from Rouault),
making of New York characteristics a Byzantine devotion to the meaning
of the objects of his regard as they appear in the world, a New York
forcefulness and objectivity of technique at the service, say, of the *Cru-
cifixion*[4] (where, by the way, his originality of palette replaces Byzantine
gold with a flat light ochre like American earth). Elaine de Kooning, on
the other hand, draws her strength from being indigenous; what elements
of abstract-expressionism remain in her work are there as accidental auto-
biography. Her basketball players leap in excitement of paint which are
like the cheerings of spectators or like the fall air in New York, vivid,
brisk, busy. What she experiences seems to go straight to the canvas,
partially due to her adroitness as a draughtsman in capturing physical
movement; the force of her perceptions obliterates stylistic effects and
sets free a plastic vitality which in the baseball and basketball pictures is
the epitome of that aspect of American life (not melodramatic, like Bel-
lows) and which, in the seated figures *Conrad* or *Willem de Kooning,* pre-
sents a composed, contemplative man in the surcharged violence of his
days. It is a mark of her vigor that not a stroke can be interpreted in rela-
tion to anything but the perception — her work does not refer back to
the artist (as an action or document does), but forward to life. Unlike Mrs.
de Kooning's, Grace Hartigan's work is a communication between the artist
and art, much of it a monologue through which the artist informs art of
her insights into nature; the artist is of necessity present as narrator, in
much the same way that Franz Kline is present in his work as the medium
of its violence. She began as an abstract painter and her history is interest-
ing in relation to what I have said about the siren-like call of nature to

young painters. Miss Hartigan was in what a Japanese might call "The Painters Workshop" of the New York School, showed in the 9th Street Show and the New Talent Show at the Kootz Gallery; her early work shows the influence of Hans Hofmann's teachings and Jackson Pollock's free, iconoclastic spirit. She is said to have awakened one morning to the desicion that she could paint abstractly no longer. At any rate, return to nature meant going forward to new territory in art, for what historically may be called a return was for her a first approach. She put behind her the exclusively esthetic concerns of her abstractions, her new canvases erupting with images and influences hitherto repressed: fantastic nudes and constumed figures, loaded still lifes like rock quarries, overt references to the monumental bathers of Cézanne and Matisse as well as to the *Demoiselles d'Avignon* period of Picasso. She had found that the great, beautiful and solitary aim of abstract painting was not hers, she could not give enough to that art. Essentially a painter of heterogeneous pictures which bring together wildly discordant images through insight into their functional relationship (their "being together in the world"), her method is seen in bold relief next an abstract painter like Philip Guston, for instance, whose varied periods and explorations culminate in the pure, unified and perfect silence of his present work. From Miss Hartigan's early work to her latest one notes the progress of inclusion, a continual effort to put more into the picture without sacrificing the clarity she loves in Matisse nor subduing the noise of the desperate changes she perceives in the world around her. Her paintings are full of nerves and senses: the *River Bathers*,[5] a traditionally pastoral subject, quivers with the apprehension of sunlight and cold water on tender flesh, the *Ocean Bathers*[6] is blindingly hot and stinging. She retains the chaotic brushwork and whirling impasto of expressionism, but in turning to nature she has introduced a passion which was only implied in the early work — the sombre *Massacre* with its elegantly serious contortions gives way to the tragic *Masquerade* where the individual identities are being destroyed by costumes which imprison them, and to the *Grand Street Brides,* who face without bitterness the glassy shallowness of American life which is their showcase.

In these three painters we find the dual play of response to nature and desire for plastic organization setting up a friction which may be the dramatic meaning of the pictures, especially in Mr. De Niro and Miss Hartigan, both of whom cling to theoretical stylistic considerations not found in, say, Jane Freilicher's work, and the which adds a consciously artistic undercurrent to their main preoccupations.

The paintings of Jane Freilicher are imbued with modesty, grace and
subtlety; she has eschewed the brilliant effects of much contemporary
painting in favor of a rendering of what she perceives in nature. Her earlier
work was involved with what she felt toward the subject; always inspired
by nature, she employed a youthful automatism based on delight in her
feelings (while painting a reclining figure,[7] she would lie down to "feel"
the form). But the act of painting is not glamorous to her. She shies away
from surface excitement, finding it too easy, which is to say too soon.
The composer Ben Weber once remarked that composing was "a great
and tedious responsibility"; Miss Freilicher's responsibility seems to be to
her perceptions rather than to painting — the originality of her color, for
instance, comes not from stylistic concern with its concomitant emphasis
on intelligence but from a sensibility liberated from self-consciousness by
its intense occupation with what it perceives and means. In this connec-
tion, one might cite Milton's "Lycidas," where the subject (a friend's pre-
mature death by drowning) has freed the poet's sensibility from the rather
arch stylistic considerations of many other poems of that period. Stylistic
preoccupation often makes for sameness, the trap of the look, of perform-
ance. There is an initial perception which becomes a method: the percep-
tion of what painting is, or how it is done, and that is a great pleasure but
it is not the highest art can afford. We like to think that an opera singer or
a pianist will sustain the level of execution through successive perform-
ances — that is not what we hope for the painter.

The abnegation by the artist of this delight in performance is age-old.
It is returning to us in America, perhaps, via the Orient — Chinese and
Japanese art, Zen Buddhism. One of Lady Murasaki's[8] characters (circa
A.D. 1000) offers a timely discussion: "In the Painters Workshop too
there are many excellent artists chosen for their proficiency in ink-
drawing; and indeed they are all so clever it is hard to set one above the
other. But all of them are at work on subjects intended to impress and
surprise. One paints the Mount of Horai; another a raging sea-monster
riding a storm; another, ferocious animals from the Land beyond the sea,
or faces of imaginary demons. Letting their fancy run wildly riot they have
no thought of beauty, but only of how best they may astonish the be-
holder's eye. And though nothing is real, all is probable. But ordinary hills
and rivers, just as they are, houses such as you may see anywhere, with all
their real beauty and harmony of form — quietly to draw such scenes as
this, or to show what lies beyond some intimate hedge that is folded away
far from the world, and thick trees upon some unheroic hill, and all this

with befitting care for composition, proportion, and the like — such works demand the highest master's utmost skill and must needs draw the common craftsman into a thousand blunders." I don't mean to minimize the artistic value of the bravura style by referring thus to a sensibility which is more general in the East — no one who loves the music of Liszt or the painting of Kandinsky can deny the role of vigor and brilliance in Western art. But my quotation does point to a contemporary attitude which is potentially dangerous, the attitude that a quieter gift signifies a "minor" sensibility not standing up to the challenges of bravura execution, that the return to the figure and nature in American painters signifies a falling away from passion, from profundity. Nor is the work of these younger painters (though Miss Freilicher's recent landscapes and still lifes are very close to the spirit of the quotation) restricted to such scenes as the Japanese adore. Distinguished in pastel as in oil, she brings an original formal gift which is rigorously removing all extraneous utterance from her identifications with the inexorable calm of nature's movements.

The painting of Larry Rivers hints at psychological perception, though it is not precisely that, since its technical resources refer more to the Renaissance "psychology of art" than to contemporary scientific-humanist curiosity. It is painting "in"; nothing is left for the eye to put together, as there is in impressionism, even in his earliest paintings, the ones that resembled Renoir and Bonnard. What in the impressionists was broken up so the eye would join it together again was an end in itself to Mr. Rivers and represented the deliciousness of painting. To dab and fling directly on the canvas is to impose color on a white surface, to compose a picture which is only partially (clumsily to the realist) apprehended by the eye is a way of asserting the deliciousness of painting over the deliciousness of skillful representation, over the subject and its individual objects, over nature and life itself. Later, through the sometime influences of Soutine and Robert De Niro (whose show at the Egan Gallery in 1950 gave inspiration and permission to many young painters in their attempt to escape the mannerisms of abstract impressionism), Mr. Rivers' stroke became wider, the paint thicker and more Fauve, the images were flung even more joyously and carelessly, the surface had air and depth, vivacity and solidity. But simultaneously, as if to take up this fiercer style were to be cursed with the cares of the *peintres maudits* who originated it, his subject matter took on a new seriousness, notably in *The Burial,*[9] a grand conception inspired by Courbet, whom he studied more and more. Appropriately enough this period was one of intense interest in Willem de Koon-

ing's figures and where Mr. Rivers' drawing had been free it became fierce;
where it had been spontaneous it became conceptualized; the painting,
where before it had described an airy all-over surface which was more im-
portant than the figures it partially revealed, now presented drawing-in-
paint, figures undifferentiated from their ground, savage arabesques of
harsh multilinear power without feature or character, whose modus vi-
vendi lay entirely in the paint, often brutally vulgar (*Woman with Hair-
curlers*,[10] for instance, with its greasy lipstick smile and calico house-
dress), sometimes tender and culminating in the *Two Women Posing*[11]
(in which the figures are almost absorbed in the delicate hues of a land-
scape which continually comes forward into the female forms) and in a
portrait of myself[12] through which he came to the decision that the fig-
ure is divorced from its background, thus solving a difficulty which neither
Courbet nor de Kooning had helped him with. Though this decision is
perhaps closer to the Renaissance than to either, he felt that it satisfied
the requirements of what he saw in nature and what he sought in painting,
without recourse to stylistic overstroking, slashing or obtrusive drawing.
This decision initiated a period of sculpture and of close observation of
nature. The paintings that came from it make drawing the hero, further
emphasized by a muted palette, and although these works are somewhat
reminiscent of Pascin, especially in the pictures of *Mrs. Bertha Burger*,[13]
they are closer, I think, to the abstract implications of Cézanne, notably
in the *Watermill Prospect*[14] and the monumental *Self Figure*.[15] Pushing
this decision even further, and as his grasp of realistic representation in
sculpture increased, a mastery of formal effect in painting followed which
is based on perception of natural light and anatomy in the Renaissance
"studio" manner (as opposed to Miss Freilicher's "plein air" feeling) and
which is at its height in the beautiful paint applications and slightly im-
posed waves of melancholy in the recent *Widow of Sidney Burger*.

   One may say that Mr. Rivers found in nature what he sought in art,
turning to the subject itself rather than to the various manners of ap-
proaching the subject. This is even truer of the still lifes of Felix Pasilis;
all of his paintings "work" in the Hofmann sense, but this compositional
skill is like handwriting in his pictures, completely at the service of the
meaning of the work, at the service of his brooding, violent meditations
on the essential quality of the coffee pots, flowers and stepladders as
they assert themselves in light and in space, full to overflowing with color
and with sentiment. Using a heavy impasto to weight the relationships of
his subtly perceived masses from which flowers burst forth and into which

light seems to seep as you look, he captures the felicity of inanimate objects as they are, implying that effortlessness Proust attributes to an Elstir watercolor — "(it) gave me that particular kind of enchantment which is diffused by works of art not only deliciously executed but representing a subject so singular and so seductive that it is to it that we attribute a great deal of their charm, as if the charm were something that the painter had merely to uncover, to observe, realised already in a material form by nature, and to reproduce in art . . . " and again, " . . . nothing in this watercolor was merely stated there as a fact and painted because of its utility to the composition . . ." This is the gift lauded by our Japanese gentleman and its appearance now in New York is an event, this discovery of the innate quality of the mass which so heightens the effect of Mr. Pasilis' extraordinarily original sense of color. How often in Kandinsky (but not in Mondrian) we feel the impulse of the color strongly at first only to have it disappear later in the welter of architectonics, appearing and disappearing *artificially* by virtue of the artist's sophisticated juxtaposition of relationships. Mr. Pasilis' colors stand forth boldly, singly, naturally, independent of all but the light itself in their vital burst.

Like most of the artists discussed here, Wolf Kahn enjoys the wide frame of reference which painting nature enjoins. In a way, it is the prolongation of sensation into the future; you see, you absorb, you perceive, you paint, you see anew. Mr. Kahn has the sensibility of the impressionists — not just their vision, their design, their science; he sees impressionistically, especially in his earlier work. He sees millions of colors on each leaf, he sees light breaking over a face like foam, he sees an eye rolling in an abyss of pearly hues, he sees the sun shedding its gold over the landscape like blood. It is the measure of his strength that this seeing finds its structure, too, in nature, pressing as Soutine and Van Gogh did the intelligibility to appear no matter how rigorous the price. His paintings are very beautiful and very serious; very rich and very sad; very bright and very heavy. Like the passion of a Svengali for a Trilby, he seems to brood over nature at the same time as he presents its exquisite moments. The structure of the picture takes on personal strength and openness, as if an intimate secret were being divulged, with a warning. His self-portraits[16] of a year ago make this quality quite apparent: the artist is depicted in a bold emotional state, beset on every side by cutting colors, some sweeping into his form, others approaching and passing with the speed of arrows, and his eyes are everywhere upon them. These pictures brought a new personal feeling which is less to do with what he appreciates and more to do with what he perceives. At the same time they have an objectivity of emotional statement within the stance which is like a date under a Romantic poem: you read a fervent farewell, and the footnote tells you the poet died the next morning at Missolonghi. The "genuineness" of the paintings, their forms and details, no matter what the influence, has that kind of extraneous, compelling conviction — his *Still Life With Sting Ray*[17] is overtly Soutinesque and yet very cold and light; his pastels are so French in color, yet so geometrically perceived; the lavishly painted landscapes and dune pictures have the pleasure of a scream from a well-trained soprano, but it is still nevertheless a scream and as such is more natural than singing. In the most recent paintings a new particularization of seen detail and of paint application makes the range abrupt within small areas; a dune-house interior flooded with darkness which seems caused by the hot sunlight outside the door treats the eye much the way nature does, careless of sudden shocks. In front of one of Mr. Kahn's paintings one is not always in command of oneself or of the experience, and as one sees longer it becomes apparent that an unknown quantity of perception is available to one's flagging powers, as in nature the hidden secret is partially revealed — or else this is the mysterious quality of painting itself.

So nature is with us? These new painters have done what they had to do and found what painting seemed to need for them. They have no group, they mail no manifestos and, unlike the surrealists or magic realists or academicians, they do not favor a given look or an external content; they do not separate themselves from painting.

Notes:

1. Willem de Kooning, *Excavation,* Art Institute of Chicago.
2. Willem de Kooning, *Woman,* Museum of Modern Art, New York.
3. Robert De Niro, *Woman with a Parasol,* Collection Barbara Guest.
4. Robert De Niro, *Crucifixion,* Museum Purchase Fund.
5. Grace Hartigan, *River Bathers,* Museum of Modern Art.
6. Grace Hartigan, *Ocean Bathers,* Collection Mr. and Mrs. Jay Steinberg, Chicago.

7. Jane Freilicher, *Reclining Figure,* Collection John Latouche.

8. Lady Murasaki, *The Tale of Genji,* translated by Arthur Waley.

9. Larry Rivers, *The Burial,* Museum Purchase Fund.

10. Larry Rivers, *Woman with Haircurlers,* Collection Kenward Elmslie.

11. Larry Rivers, *Two Women Posing,* reproduced by *Art News,* December 1952.

12. Larry Rivers, *Portrait of Frank O'Hara,* Collection William S. Lieberman.

13. Fairfield Porter, "Rivers Paints a Picture," *Art News,* January 1954.

14. Larry Rivers, *Watermill Prospect,* Collection James Merrill.

15. Larry Rivers, *Self Figure,* Collection Ben Heller.

16. Wolf Kahn, *Self Portrait,* reproduced by *Art News,* November 1953.

17. Wolf Kahn, *Still Life with Sting Ray,* Collection Nell Blaine.

[*Folder* 3, 1954]

PORTER PAINTS A PICTURE

Fairfield Porter lives in Southampton, Long Island, a town which looks
permanent for all its handsomeness and rather reminds you of Henry
James — unlike some of the other Hamptons which resemble watering
places, beautiful but fleeting, and remind you of Scott Fitzgerald. There's
no house in Southampton that's supposed to have been Gatsby's.

Porter's rambling white house (the effect is increased by the garage
and the barn-studio not adjoining but fanning out across the back of his
property, like a tail) is Jamesian, too: its many rooms invite and impose
privacy to a degree; and the soft light, result of elms far and high enough
to subdue the sun without really shading the house, lends subtlety to faded
walls held in place by Japanese prints, Audubon birds and early de Koonings.

Porter has been painting for twenty-five years, though not always inten-
sively. His duties as a critic for *Art News* have brought him in to New York
once a month for the past three years, and this literary activity has led him
to formulate his ideals of painting very clearly: he doesn't try to find what
he does best, but to do what he finds best in painting. There is a difference,
I think, between a method based on natural inclination and one based on
conscious aim, the difference perhaps between Mozart and Berlioz. "I want
to do everything that avant-garde theoreticians say you can't do. When
someone says you can't disregard the past fifty years of art history, it makes
me want to prove you can — the avant-garde implies a protocol which is
more a challenge than a guide. Not that the Academicians aren't even more
ignorant!" With such definite ideas about the historical as well as esthetic
position of the artist, one finds Porter (like Henry James, again) both ob-
jective and prejudiced.

Though he studied art history at Harvard and later learned things about
drawing and composition, under Boardman Robinson and Thomas Benton
at the Art Students League, nobody taught anything about painting itself
which he felt he, as a student, could use. What help he got from others
came mostly from conversations with van Hooten, a Belgian painter he met
while copying a Tiepolo in the Metropolitan, and with Willem de Kooning.
Both had insights into the craft of painting that were useful and inspiring
to Porter, who has always wanted to be "a painter, not just an artist." His
interest in craftsmanship led him to investigate the discoveries of Maroger,
whose "Venetian" medium he has used for several years.

A week after his second one-man show opened at the Tibor de Nagy

Gallery in New York last year, Porter decided to start a portrait of his daughter, Katharine, who is four-and-a-half years old, already a gifted poet (her work resembles that of Theodore Roethke) and great lady (when asked if her name should be spelled Kitty or Katy for this article, she said coolly, "My name is Katharine"). Previous attempts to paint her had either "not worked out" or failed because of the difficulty of getting a child to pose. She was more docile now, and this seemed a good way to begin painting again after the distractions of the exhibition. She posed in a large wing-chair upholstered with a flowered pattern on a field of dark brown; her mother stayed nearby to read to her when she grew restless.

Composition, for Porter, is a conscious procedure, an advance of decisions which become more and more irrevocable as the work goes on: the subject (its size and position), the area around it to be included, color and its differentiation, linear continuity and similarity, distinctions of mass, these things are arrived at gradually through detailed decisions. But no part of the picture is finished before another: "it should always have a look of beginning, of freshness"; and if a decision gives an area too much resolution, it is removed or altered.

He did a number of sketches of his daughter in her chair so he would know pretty well what he was doing when he approached the picture proper; these sketches were not of details, nor was his concern that of the draftsman. Each sketch was a whole composition, though in each case he learned something about a different part of what would be the final picture. In the first pencil sketch, for instance, he has a likeness in the face which he did not "get" in any of the later sketches, but he had not yet decided to use the left wing of the chair. Similarly, in his second oil sketch a necessary expansion of the chair's form followed from his attention to the details of the pattern on it (in the earlier oil sketch he had first drawn the outlines of the chair and from then on the forms within it tended to look cramped). By the time he had completed this series of sketches, two in pencil and two in oil, he had his motif definitely in mind. The canvas proper would be an attempt to execute this image according to the dictates of his taste with little or no element of "painting as discovery" or of subconscious revelation as we know it in "action-painting" or expressionism. Nor would there be any but the most incidental formal discoveries to be made, since Porter takes an almost moral stand against the accidental once he has a given painting consciously in hand.

The necessity for being so thoroughly prepared to begin a painting is, of course, personal and specific (he does not invariably work this way), but in

Porter's case the necessity has been made more immediate by his using the
Maroger medium, a medium which enables one to work wet, to erase easily,
to blend colors "in" and to use the underlayers of paint as a presence
which is not completely canceled by painting over. At the same time, the
Maroger medium is peculiarly unsuited to those who do not know what they
want at the outset, since if it is fussed with or changed too much it gets rub-
bery and unpleasant. If all the decisions were to occur on the canvas, as they
often do in action-painting, the medium might work against the inspiration
of the artist in the picture's final stages.

But when an artist already knows what he wants, this medium helps him
to do it and allows a few mistakes, erasures and adjustments while retaining
the fresh surface quality. Many of Porter's paintings have a look of spon-
taneity and effortless felicity, an anonymous and silent placidity of the
paint itself.

For the first two sketches the subject posed diligently; after that posing
was intermittent. One pencil sketch is a good likeness, and the space to the
left of the chair seems to push the figure into the chair arm in a way that
suggests the vacant pressures of introspection, but this psychological effect
was abandoned for what Porter could actually observe when he came to
the following sketches. For the first oil sketch he used sized canvas but did
not spread it with medium first, as is often done, because it makes colors
blend more than he wanted them to. He preferred a thinner paint quality
than wet-in-wet permits. Instead, he merely mixed his tube colors with
medium and applied them direct, drawing with the brush, a No. 16 sable
(he also uses oxhair and bristle brushes, finding oxhair a nice mean between
bristle stiffness and sable softness). The actual colors and forms present in
life were noted: brown chair with red flowers, blonde girl in pink sweater
and rose dress. The second oil sketch began with pale washes while the sub-
ject decided whether she wished to pose or not. As her mother read to her,
she began to appear on the canvas, her dress pink, her sweater cream, seat-
ed in a greenish grey chair surrounded by wet white space; then her dress
became brighter — red. The model left. Having noted the actual colors in
the first sketch, Porter now felt free to explore the color distinctions as
they related to the composition becoming more definite in his eyes. In con-
centrating on details of the chair's patterned upholstery, the form expanded.
He put the floor under the chair and drew a mantel to the right with tur-
pentine and black paint; the details of the mantel fitted unobtrusively into
the surface because it had medium already on it (drawing can be the last
thing, using this medium, as in Tiepolo).

In appraising these two sketches, Porter found that the first had the fussiness of attempted accuracy, the second more differences. The wall and the skin of the face, though, were too like in color so he deepened the whitish wall with a little vermilion and black and it began to go further back, thus offering another distinction of tone. In preparing for the final painting, he increased the detail of his perception rather than his perception of details, accomplishing this largely through distiction of mass. He relies neither on spontaneity nor on originality of viewpoint. He does not paint a version of reality: there is something there which he can get "right" in art, with perseverance, insight and luck. "Art is the perception of differences rather than likenesses," but it is also involved in preserving the appearance of things so that these distinctions do not occur in a vacuum.

Porter is tall and energetic, with abrupt mannerisms which make his silence as foreceful as his speaking. He is boyish in his eagerness for facts, facts of any variety from any source: no specialist in a field anywhere from atomic fission to roulette systems could have a more avid listener. When he can, though, he prefers to work at a thing himself: he doesn't just read essays on Mallarmé, he does English versions of the poems himself. Painting is his way of working at nature. He imitates nature not to resemble it but to appreciate and understand it. Some artists wish to *be* nature; Porter does not, and he is not much moved by accidents, even symbolic ones, in nature. What he pursues in his imitation of nature is composition.

Composition is a function of the sensibility; it is the personal statement of the insight which observation and insight afford. It is also an "agreement for cessation of hostilities" (*Concise Oxford Dictionary*) between oneself and nature. It is not an illusion as is the expression of an experience, as is the representation of observation; when composition is weighted so heavily with an almost symbolic importance, it deviates sharply from what we recognize as composition in an expressionist or realist painting. Fairfield Porter's paintings stand or fall by their composition: it is the literal meaning of his perceptions and he will do any number of versions of a motif to perfect its utterance. Perhaps it is only his insistence on presenting differences within the compositional perception which keeps his paintings from becoming abstractions and therefore facts, in the sense that a Mondrian is a fact. He is interested in the areas of forms, rather than their contours, and it is in the interior quality of areas that the distinctions between forms become most clear. He has never, to my knowledge, painted an arabesque.

The impressionists had the sensibility for this interior quality to a re-
markable degree, but they tended to give up sensibility in favor of con-
struction, to become a fact: Mondrian is the obvious outgrowth of this ten-
dency. The action-painters, on the other hand, perpetuate impressionist sen-
sibility (the impressionists were "action painters") and they are not inter-
ested in the distinctions which composition itself presents: they wish to *be*
nature, and to this extent their paintings accomplish accidental composition
based on likenesses rather than differences. Porter finds Vuillard and Bon-
nard at the intersection of these two tendencies. They compose with the
sensibility for interior qualities of the impressionists, and they are the re-
cent masters he most admires.

Before beginning *Portrait of Katharine*, Porter did a second pencil
sketch, taking care to note details of living-room wall and fireplace as well
as the curves of the chair and continuities of line (from chair leg up left wall
of fireplace, from chair back into mantel-molding, and so on); these were
the properties of drawing, the contours, which he got so he could lose them
in the actual painting.

In drawing with charcoal on the big canvas, his rough outline of the forms
was based on actual measurement of the chair and the model: "An aunt of
mine who had studied with Eakins said something that always stuck in my
head — she was looking at a portrait and remarked, 'It's that terribly unfor-
tunate size, slightly smaller than life.' I certainly want to avoid that." He did
not coat the canvas with medium, fearing that a wet look in the beginning
would result in a vaseline look at the end. Of the two Maroger mediums,
Porter uses the Venetian rather than the Flemish; it is less shiny, calling for
wax where the latter requires mastic varnish. In preparing the formula, he
melts beeswax over a low heat, adding one to three teaspoons of ammonia
per pound of beeswax (excess ammonia volatilizes); the recipe calls for one
part of this prepared beeswax, one part lead carbonate (white lead) and ten
parts raw linseed oil, which must be stirred over a fire to keep the lead and
beeswax from settling, and must not exceed 250 degrees centigrade — it is
both poisonous and inflammable and may foam up below this temperature,
when it should be removed for a time. In about an hour the mixture turns
the color of Italian coffee. After it cools it may be stored in jars; by this time
it is the color of American coffee, though transparent when combined with
pigments or spread on canvas. Porter mixes the medium with pigments be-
forehand. White lead is mixed with it, too, even when it will be used in com-
bination with pigments which already have medium in them. The pigments
are "suspended" in the medium; they stay brighter and one can use a color

like vermilion without risk of its turning black.

He first fixed the chair by indicating its surroundings: white wash for mantelpiece, pink back wall, light ocher floor. The chair and figure went untouched, he always must fix the subject in space first — "I always do it, I can't help it. I have to know where the thing is. Once when I was in a mechanical-drawing class I was supposed to design a machine. After getting the working parts, I put in the parts they joined, then I added the surface it was on, and the legs of the table, and the walls and the floor and a window. . . . They threw me out. Later on, when I worked for the Navy during the war, I got over this to some extent, though."

Starting on the figure and the chair, he followed his method of keeping the paint at the same stage all over. As Kitty's dress became a deeper tone, the pattern of the chair became more definite and differentiated in the flowers and the background; the floor beneath the chair began to go back and the wall took on an angle toward the mantel, this rear wall deepening as Kitty's face looked like a little three-quarter moon. "I want the painted-*in* quality," he said: "everything of equal value, the darkest corner as valuable as the brightest lip or eye. Provincial painting doesn't have this, it rushes toward an artistic end, not realizing that in art every means is the end. I don't want anything coming out of the picture." At several stages he was forced to lose passages of interest to keep the painting "fresh" all over — one being a perfect likeness of the sitter's face which gave that area a prematurely finished look. One day he drew with charcoal over the painted areas, first rubbing the face out down to the canvas; the next he covered the whole with medium. The drawing sank into the canvas, he began working wet, drawing the features of the face with a sable brush in black, marking the wall and floor more definite, putting casters on the chair legs. The figure in its dark red dress and pink sweater, hands in repose, feet tucked up, gave him least trouble of all, but a likeness in the face would not come. The chair pattern meanwhile had become smudged and quiet, like old brocade. Returning to the living-room where his daughter had posed he noted a drawing she had done of one of her dolls, a blue pack of cards, a red pack; they were on the mantel and solved an emptiness he had felt there. By just placement of the eyes and lips the face suddenly resembled the sitter without giving the area a definition too articulate for the aim of the picture as a whole. Now the more "drawn" details in mantel-molding and baseboard provided contrast to the subtle paint transitions of the larger forms, giving a directional emphasis — like a doorway in a Bonnard, or a band of flat paint in a de Kooning interior.

Speaking of Porter when this and other pictures of his were exhibited
in a group show at East Hampton this summer, a Dante scholar and afi-
cionado of contemporary painting remarked: "It is very clear and strong,
this sensibility, but not just that. Seen here, along with others of the New
York School, it is not at variance with any principle; it is distinct but not
argumentative; and one can see it advancing into the future, not subject
to decay."

Portrait of Katharine glows like a pearl with that luminous greyness
which is the hero of much contemporary painting, its ultimate differ-
entiations melting into each other and then reappearing, like the veinings
of leaves in late afternoon as the wind calmly stirs them.

[*Art News,* January 1955]

ANOTHER WORD ON KENNETH KOCH

> *"Mr. Koch, it seems, has a rare combination of words rattling about in his skull, but it is difficult to call any of his word combinations the bric-a-brac of poetry."*
> — Harry Roskolenko, *Poetry,* July 1954

It is amusing to think of the number of gifted (even great!) poets my epigraph applies to. Though I am in total disagreement with the rest of Mr. Roskolenko's review of *Poems* by Kenneth Koch (Tibor de Nagy Gallery Editions), he has hit on something here; these very original poems have little to do with the restful and pleasant bric-a-brac he seems to prefer (he recommends the satire of another poet, finally, on the grounds that "no one will be actually offended").

Mr. Koch's poems have a natural voice, they are quick, alert, instinctive and, within the limited scope of this first volume, indicate a potentially impressive variety. His technique is opposed to that Academic and often turgid development by which many young poets gain praise for their "achievement," an achievement limited usually to the mastery of one phase of Yeats (and usually the last). This is not to say that these poems do not have their precedents, but Mr. Koch intends to "make it new" —

> Once again I find the charge accounts
> and remedies not enough. You have borrowed my gas range,
> And the steep prunes of my kiss
> Must leave you within the graceless forest
> Garbage garage charm-account.

Mr. Roskolenko writes, "He is precious and puerile when he is not merely futile and noisy . . ."; but there is another way of reading the work. Poetry in our times may be distinguished without being frozen. I find Koch close to the light sensuality of the Cavalier poets; there is a debt, too, to those catalogues of Whitman in which the poet warmly embraces the vulgar and inanimate objects of everyday life and to the syntactical abbreviations in early Auden. Most prominent as an influence is the verbal playfulness and irony we find in recent French poets like Raymond

Roussel, Benjamin Péret, Henri Michaux, Raymond Queneau (the latter's
infatuation with American oddities of custom and terminology finds a
native echo in this book) as well as in our own Theodore Roethke. Is

>   We drank the iced tea, then
>   Moved our ship slowly out to sea
>   While the Infant was blasting the rose,
>   O love was the engine

or

>   Ah, she was a tall, slim girl
>   Not made for either office-work or repose.

precious in a pejorative sense? I think not. Not the least function of
poetry is to make vivid our sense of the meaning of words. He tends to
enlarge where others narrow down. Words need not be purified until the
tribe has sullied them; after two generations of continual washing it is a
wonder words have any color left. I do not wish to make false claims for
Mr. Koch: he will undoubtedly not, from the indications of this volume,
write a Gray's "Elegy." He has the other poetic gift: vivacity and go,
originality of perception and intoxication with life. Most important of all,
he is not *dull*.

But rather than describe my own pleasure in the work, here is a speech
from scene 5 of the play, *Pericles*, in which the technical glitter enhances
a characteristically positive emotional statement.

>   There's no midnight mystery
>   and no coconuts here to see,
>   nothing but the ocean's sea
>   which will wash history's tattoos from me;
>   I hope to live satisfactorily
>   like a capon that's struck by a tree
>   and does die gladly
>   bereft, O large, of his sexuality,
>   Oh as honey fills the bee
>   while the waves' orchestra's business spree
>   sticks its night in your head like a country,
>   and as the madman throws the flea

to music, helplessly,
here always shall I be
and not in idolatry,
but yet superfluous as a ski
on a barge; while the withered air
reduces baneful boughs to everywhere.

[*Poetry,* March 1955]

ON AND ON ABOUT KENNETH KOCH:
A COUNTER-REBUTTAL

Since I do not believe that "poetry is still a matter of private taste" but
rather one of public responsibility, I am dissatisfied with Mr. Roskolenko's
rebuttal to my remarks on Kenneth Koch's *Poems, Poetry* June 1955. The
main point against what he calls my "variety of literary follies" seems to
be that Mr. Koch could not possibly be influenced by the poets I name be-
cause he is not, in his first book, superior to any or all of them, "in one
fell radiation."

Who ever said he was? I do not read in the rebuttal any perception of
qualities in the influences I claim which would make them antithetical to
Mr. Kock's work, on the other hand. Where in his original writing about
the book he misrepresented the poems, he now proceeds to misrepresent
me and by the way several poets I had the temerity to mention. "What
gall" indeed. As an instance, I said nothing about Whitman or Auden in
general, but about the catalogues in one and the syntactical abbreviations
in the other, both of which Mr. Koch does just happen to resemble in
several of his poems. I qualified other influences, too, and certainly was
not computing the relative statures of any poets cited. If a little anthology
of what Mr. Koch's work resembles would be helpful, it can be easily
drawn from these poets. I was thinking of specific poems and devices in
them.

But the important issue, I think, is not that Mr. Roskolenko dislikes
Mr. Koch's work, but that the principles he so dearly guards in doing it
are stultifying and arbitrary. Poems are not mature, nor are they childish.
I do not believe that analogies to cooking help much, either. Poetry is ex-
perience, often peculiar to the poet. The formal values to which, for con-
venience and expediency, we attempt to ascribe the qualities we admire
in a poem are, after all, no more than conveniences. It should be under-
stood that they are signs for the qualitites, not absolute rules by which
the work is judged. They have nothing to do with the poem ultimately,
they are only the language in which we have fallen into the habit of dis-
cussing it, they have to do with us. My idea in writing about Mr. Koch's
poems was that this language seemed to have gotten into the way of the
work: Mr. Roskolenko's review was suddenly talking about childishness
and maturity and responsibility. This was a disservice to poetry.

An example of what I mean is the 2nd paragraph of his rebuttal. Since when have poems been cooked of "verbal excitement," "significant detail," "tension," "inventive imagery"? You may find qualities in a poem and discuss them in these clichés, but a great poem can exist without a single one of them no matter how many "angles" you look at it from (an interesting exercise, by the way).

Again, if a poem exists, what difference does it make how old its poet is? The whole conundrum about children's art is completely passé — in the other arts Satie, Dubuffet and many others have accepted spontaneity and freedom from formalistic constraints to their benefit, basing their works in some cases on children's drawings, the work of the insane and aural or visual accidents. The public is far from lax in appreciating the special qualitites this liberation has permitted, but apparently news is slow to reach Mr. Roskolenko. Infantilism has many forms.

Finally, I have read and reread the excerpts from Mr. Koch's book that Mr. Roskolenko quotes to confound me and I find my initial enthusiasm for them not a whit dimmed by the god wots that surround them.

[Henry Rago of *Poetry* returned this with a note: "I don't think we can carry the debate any further. I think we've hit just the right pitch of interest and we should stop there." Ed.]

ABOUT BEN WEBER

Like so many of the most eminent artists of our time, Ben Weber has found an audience for his music slowly and gradually. His sensibility is restricting and his whole approach to the problem of creating art is one of attempting an ever more truthful, and thus more difficult, simplicity. His audience is made up of those who feel an individual response to this sensibility. He has at no time composed in a manner which could be taken up or championed by one of the various groups of musical interests: the atonalists cannot find him consistently atonal; the use of twelve-tone technique is entirely dependent on his personal needs at the time of writing; and the formal shape his movements often take, far from being based on a feeling for neoclassicism, is merely the technical (that is, external) simplicity which his complex insights and intentions choose to become as the details merge into the whole. (Willem de Kooning once remarked, "I think I'm painting a picture of two women but it may turn out to be a landscape.") The audience is not considered in this process any more than a given style is, for the creation of art is an integral part of the life function and Weber tries to curb irrelevancies of energy or of talent; while art is done *for* others as well as for oneself, it is not done *to* them, their needs must not be confused with the needs of the artistic process. Or put in another way, Weber's own words, "People who are depending on posterity pretend to themselves that what is important to people they will never know is important to them. This puts off the problem, which is an early one, of deciding upon your talent, not because people like what you do, but because you are a person of discrimination and taste and know what you create."

His attitude in respect to the audience is one rare among contemporary American artists, for whom the desire to please and to be significant and to be felt has always been the great temptation. Weber has somehow, in the midst of our difficult and obscure position as artists in America, found the courage and the strength to adhere to a strict esthetic. He has never permitted his artistic vigilance to relax into any of the interests such relaxation may adopt in our times without general disapprobation: he has not been more than conversationally diverted by the "wholesomeness and inventiveness" of popular forms or the chic of slightly dated ones; the importance which the physical experience of his life has held for the impetus of his music has never led him into anthropo-musical or exotic atmospheres; nowhere in his work can we find the principle of diversion at its dispersive tasks. He always writes as directly as possible. What he comes up with is a consistently poetic tone in his compositions and a serious emotional comment.

About the act of composing itself Weber has said, in answer to a question on the nature of his introspective process put by Lou Harrison, "Probably the process of introspection which governs most of my personal existence is very closely related to the impulses of perception which prompt me to write music. No more than many composers, and possibly much less than some, do I enjoy the act of composing itself. It seems to me a great and tedious responsibility. Every now and then, however, consistently I might say, I am moved to write music which seems inevitable to me. I do not mean to imply any particular mystic reception, but rather to state that it is necessary for me to write the works that I do in order to accomplish emotional comfort.

Ben Weber's first pieces take their departure from the *Piano Pieces, Opus 19*, of Arnold Schoenberg and works of similar mood and scope by Schoenberg and his disciples. Weber had just left pre-medical studies at the University of Illinois and was in a state of high dissatisfaction; he returned to Chicago, where he studied musical theory at De Paul University and wrote his early pieces, many of them, because of his friendship with the cellist, Seymour Barab, for cello and piano. Before coming to New York in 1945, he prepared twenty-one works because he felt that it would not be the right atmosphere for beginning new works immediately; almost all of these pieces have been given here since. He was able, after his arrival in New York, to continue to spend much of his time and energy exclusively on music and it is interesting to note here that as he has grown more ambitious towards this content, his development has reversed that of the atonal composers he admires: he has moved away from the microform expression which was his first model (Schoenberg's protest against the length and richness of Post-Romantic composers) towards a vocabulary which allows greater extension of thought and passion and more variety of texture and effect. Juan Carlos Paz, writing in *Cabalgata* in 1948, said, "The harmonic language of the composer, begun already in the *Fantasy, Opus 4,* for the violin and piano, becomes concrete, little by little, in its density and drive, making easy for him his mastery of the extensive forms; and this without the slightest hint of scholasticism; these forms are solidly based on the imperatives of musical discourse, which evolves in an expressive climate and which searches and obtains its logic outside of precon-

ceived molds, without being imposed on by some acquired dogma or by
any foreign or external circumstance."

The originality of Ben Weber's work, then, is not conceptual or tech-
nical, but rather emotional and perceptual. In contrast to the technical
innovations of John Cage, for instance, or the esthetic iconoclasm of
Morton Feldman, whose originality is one of position as well as of sound,
Weber's excursions into rarities of sensibility are accomplished by means
proceeding from our most recent traditions and applied with his own in-
dividual and inimitable taste. His *String Quartet Number 2, Opus 35* has,
in certain passages, a delicacy of sensuality not unlike that of some Ravel
compositions, yet its unification of sentiment is as total as that in Webern.
The *Blake Symphony* is almost Chassidic in its richness and dolor, but its
prosody is expressionistic and dramatic; Weber seeks to set the poetic
meaning of the text (and in this he resembles Alban Berg), rather than the
more formal and more specifically verbal brilliancies which attract Virgil
Thomson or Paul Bowles in their vocal music. The *Sonata da Camera,
Opus 31*, one of his most moving and distinctive works, offers a typical
Weber duality: based on a tone-row throughout, the three movements in-
dividually avail themselves of various formal complexities; the opening
Sarabande's slow statements are continually interrupted by passionate
digressions which occur with sufficient irregularity to avoid any feeling of
schematicism; the *Passacaglia-rondo* alternates lyric passages with percus-
sive ones and ends cadentially in two keys; in the *Rondo scherzando* free
canonic imitation is frequently used, occasionally with the violin supply-
ing missing tones in the piano's tone-row, and there is a sharp reminiscence
of the blues-coda to the first movement — yet with all this intellectual
activity inviting appreciation of its own kind, the dramatic high points of
the piece have a tense and ambiguous feeling and the broadest lyrical pas-
sages retain their obscurity somehow, so that there is at no time "brilliant"
or extrovert writing, despite the technical flare. Similarly in the *Serenade*
for Harpsichord Quartet the vivacity and wit only make the underlying
harmonic poignance the more telling; it is real "night music," the irony of
a Harlequin who sings the more beautifully when he feels unheard. As
with the *Sonata da Camera*, the effect is one.

Recently he has added two major pieces to the symphonic repertoire.
The first, a violin concerto written on invitation for the Convegno Musi-
cale of the International Society for Cultural Freedom held in Rome, May
1954, I know only in the version with piano reduction of the orchestral
parts. Even in this reduced score, the amplitude of emotional discourse and

the exquisite definition of harmonic intonation is striking. The second piece, *Prelude and Passacaglia, Opus 42*, was commissioned for the Louisville Philharmonic in 1955 and has been performed there five times. To refer back to the de Kooning quotation, the two movements of the Opus 42, in the writing, have become one landscape. It is a dark piece, rich, painful, mysterious: the opening *adagio calmando* is soon disturbed by the recognition of obscure longings in the winds and strings which, developing, make clear in fragmentary form the vigor of its motivation. Ever growing, and suddenly appearing, this recognition finds temporary rest in the *lento penseroso* introduction of the passacaglia. The nineteen variations of the passacaglia are strictly based on the tone row of the prelude and, rather than representing the organic development and extension of previous material, dramatically explore the motivation discovered in the opening passages of the prelude, sweeping to a climax which is at once a realization and a cessation of unrest. This work extends the frontier of 20th century musical consciousness, and it is the frontier of perception rather than technique. On October 3rd, after the intuitive and splendidly detailed performance accorded it by Maestro Mitropoulous and the New York Philharmonic, a previously apathetic audience was moved to cheers, and it is interesting to note that those not engaged in the ovation were moved to hiss, a compliment unusual in these days of oversophistication and disinterest.

Like the poems of Rilke in which we experience an open, complicated and knowing sentiment while we read, but when we have stopped reading realize that what has actually moved us is a mystery, in each of Ben Weber's works there is a peculiar esthetic occurrence. The emotional effect of the work is not cumulative: it is varied in the duration of the performance; then, suddenly, in the first moment of silence before the piece can be quite recognized as finished, the effect appears whole and intact and surprising; with some pieces it resembles a statement, with others merely a watching. This is a characteristic more common to poetry than to music, for we are used in poetry to having our idea of what has been going on suddenly changed by reading of the last line or even word. Music usually seeks us in a different way. Indeed, there are composers springing to mind whose work cries again and again, "I am myself!" but Ben Weber is not one of them. Rimbaud declared, *Je est un autre*. This music informs us, and its composer, of those things which we are only just able to know.

[*Bulletin of American Composers Alliance*, V:2, 1955]

ROMA

Roma is a classical ballet, but its subject is not the classicism of ballet, it is the classicism of 19th century France, its gaze turned by Romanticism towards Italy, its eyes golden with the sunset of that profoundly celebrated and profoundly understood civilization. It is not a matter of local color, of popular dances, of passion, for all life seems to partake of a general idea and to be motivated by a love which is more humanistic than personal. Thus the clear architecture of *Roma,* as formally interesting as Balanchine's more abstract ballets, full of his characteristic invention and felicity, is warm and pertinent — not a thing to be admired in itself, but a development of tone. It is everywhere rediscovering values of elegance and symmetry which are European in sentiment.

The ballet builds itself with the knowledgeability of a pyramid. The base is the corps: twelve girls and eight boys, who subdivide into sets of four girls and four boys, who join periodically to form new sets of eight and of sixteen, who occasionally take separate divertissements in threes, notably at the beginning of the tarantella where two "threes" rush on headlong to announce the evening's festivities. Above this constantly varying base, two couples rise for pas de quatre variations or differentiations of ensemble dancing, and on top of it all is the peak: Miss Leclercq and Mr. Eglevsky, who do not precisely star as we know it in Romantic ballets, but retain their strong relationship with the other members of the structure — their flights, if not earthbound by far, are engined by the close logic of the corps, giving great coherence to the piece as a whole.

Similarly, the time of *Roma* is orderly and clear. The overture, quiet and nostalgic, is an effort to remember and to arrive, as if you didn't know where you were going, but you recognized the approaches from something you'd read. On opening night during the overture a deaf lady said to her companion, "Are you enjoying it?" and those within earshot laughed out loud, so aware were they of not having arrived yet. A kind of anxiety begins, a ship to Naples is wrapped in fog; then the curtain rises on Eugene Berman's substantial set, itself a realization of high structures and low skies. You're there, in a climate rather than a place. Like Childe Harold or Stendhal, you recognize, yet you are not being shown: you are simply there. This life, these attitudes and dances, existed without you and will go on without you after you have gone. *Roma* has a feeling of continuity and age in its freshness, poised and eternal; unlike, say, *Four Temperaments,* which gives you a feeling of seeing the only performance each time, as if it were marvellously improvised for the moment and cannot be done without if you're to live. *Roma* is more a matter of choice, something you may live with the dancers, a vital, social, exhausting and vivacious exchange between you and them, like trying to keep up with an exciting conversation in a foreign language. It is not native or contemporary, it is more precious than that and more precarious. And so, even in its brightest moments, *Roma* has an undercurrent of poignancy and regret, the inexplicable melancholy of a place where you are feeling perfectly happy and do not yet know that your visa has just been cancelled. You want to belong to it, you want to stay.

There are so many elements in the ballet which share and explain what we like to think of as the most attractive aspects of "our Western heritage": the exquisite courtesy of the principals and of the corps, the corps' lively decorum, the democracy of choreography wherein the girls and boys dance as much and as brilliantly as one another, the grand simplicity of the principals as they move together and apart subtly extending each other's range of expression as in a Platonic dialogue (so much in this ballet is reciprocal!), and the bursting tarantella in which we see that for free and accomplished people gaiety cannot be vulgar.

At the same time, the piece is utterly without sentimentality. Let us say that the scene is a square in Rome where people come to meet and socialize. They obviously know it very well, the arches, the delicate railing against the sky, the small obelisque in the distance that lights up with a crown in the evening. The principals do not meet for the first time on stage, they have already been lovers before the ballet begins. They are recognized as such by the townspeople: he, a man among the boys of the city, affluent, distinguished, a Stendhal hero of experience, reticence and dash; she, a girl more beautiful than the rest, whose girlish but unmaidenly virtue is admired, whose beauty is guaranteed rather than contested by the other girls.

The lovers in *Scotch Symphony* are opposed, but these are not, and, on the other hand, they do not exclude others from their love. It has an un-Romantic logicality about it and ease. They dance with the others for brief passages and turns, they can wait to be alone. When they are offstage during the scherzo, the boys stroll obliquely in fours, their heads and necks clear, gold sashes slapping their abdomens, torsos covered with buff or lavender to mid-thigh, creating a fast, stocky look to the white legs which gleam against the railing when they turn at stage rear or lift the girls

from the solid earth. The girls flutter about in full skirts just short of knees
which dip and bend and mingle with petticoats, their bare shoulders pi-
quantly held, their heads voluble with flirtation, but very gentle: the kind
of flirting that goes on in school buses or monastery gardens. Two couples
enter for a pas de quatre, declaring their affinity for each other and the
place, obviously in excellent spirits over their respective affairs. Behind
them the others form a semicircle under the central arch, now admiring,
now accompanying with glittering half-movements like waves against a
boat. The principals rejoin them briefly, the light is failing, they hasten.
It is early evening.

Now Miss Leclercq and Mr. Eglevsky are brought on by their friends
and left alone. The adagio begins. They dance closely and intimately,
duplicating each other's thoughts with great familiarity and cordiality.
And here is one of Mr. Balanchine's most lovely inspirations: at the be-
ginning of her turns, Miss Leclercq, supported on left toe, gently lifts
her right leg through the arc of her partner's arm to rest on his wrist,
lowering her torso and head horizontal while turning to assume the in-
tense quiet of the figure on Ilaria del Carretto's tomb, rising at the end
for one of her faultless arabesques which, after the presage of death in
the full security of her partner's love, is an affirmation of the alternate
inevitabilities: continuity and change. Miss Leclercq builds and builds
during this adagio. She is never at a loss for further extension of her
technical simplicity, her repose, her radiance and candor, the wealth of
feeling in her beat. Here she has not the nobility of tragic apprehension
which she has in *Swan Lake*: it is the nobility of human comprehension.

Promenaders move in from either side for a moment as the lovers re-
gain their composure; in the passages which follow their exit Miss
Leclercq reflects on the femininity of her nature in delicate pirouettes
and turns, her hands coming to rest on Mr. Eglevsky's arm or shoulder.
They walk stage right for a moment, he whispers; she admonishes with
a raised, hushing hand and darts away, only to turn and smile ravishingly,
"You should not have spoken of it!" and lift, requiring his immediate
and grateful support. One passage in this section ends with a trumpet
call in the orchestra as, with cheerful élan of the toes, she reminds her
lover that he once served in the carabinieri, and the movement comes
to a close as she descends to his knee and is folded in his arms.

Night. Chandeliers appear, the night washing is hung out between
the arches (a wonderful stroke of Mr. Berman's) and the obelisk is lit.
As the tarantella starts two trios run on stage and the corps follows in

carnival manner, the boys vigorous in red caps, the girls in head-sails of white lace like the kerchiefs women wear on random errands to church. At a reminiscence of their adagio the principals appear in their midst and join in the carnival with stunning solo variations, Mr. Eglevsky whirling offstage, Miss Leclercq ecstatic in a circle of boys rattling tambourines. The contrapuntal ensemble of the finale, complicated by beribboned tambourines and the speed of execution, has great clarity and zest as Miss Leclercq, before a throng of dancers and colors, does supported pirouettes with tambourine, sweeping into arabesques as she strikes it again and again and the curtain falls.

Looking at Balanchine's recent ballets as essays in history and in human attitudes is interesting. *Opus 34* happens in the Germany of expressionism, where terrible events are exploited ritualistically in the vain hope that their power may be exorcised. Man's own intimate creations, white plaster statues of no determinable motivation or sex, come to life, move, intermingle – and as a sequel a young girl and boy pay with their lives for having been born for such a terrible event.

Western Symphony gets much of its bite and humor from a casual and manly humor toward frustration. It is bright and ironical, everything is fun. And the ability to move and to think fast, to be gay and admired, takes away part of the pain of living, so that the cowboy, when he loses his silly beautiful girl friend takes up the reins of his fillies and advances across the prairie smiling and remarking to himself, "That's life for you!" And the other male-and-female relationships are competitive – there is camaraderie of the sexes, but not between them. These are recognizably American attitudes Balanchine has so shrewdly perceived.

And in *Ivesiana* he focuses his attention on the traumatic aspects of American life in several telling episodes, leaving no "outs" of achievement or charm or viewpoint. Nobody escapes. In dark recesses of Central Park and on the sidewalks of New York muggings take place, pavement games turn into brutal dominations, "cool" existential dance-addicts sluff off their feelings and shrug away their passions, but don't get away with it. They are all brought literally to their knees without even the blessings of metaphor by the final curtain. It's a very dark look at where we are, as shocking and depressing as it is beautiful and convincing. And simplifying this way doesn't violate the "danceness" of these ballets too much, for Balanchine's work is always inviolate and intact.

Ivesiana, for all that it is diametrically opposed to *Roma* in meaning, has one characteristic in common with the later work. *Roma,* too, is a

general statement. There are no personalities as such. The differentiation
between the two main dancers and the corps is kept to a minimum. They
dance bigger and fuller and faster, but not differently. They interpret the
steps of the corps with something added, with reflection and understand-
ing, as if they were spokesman for the tribe; they are part of society, they
exist in and because of the corps as lovers did in the 19th century and don't
any more. They may exit solo but they enter with their peers or are beheld
in their midst, bowing. Even in the adagio, one of the loveliest of pas de
deux, the soloists are reminded at the moment of impending intimacy that
they are not alone. Society has not threatened or interrupted, it has merely
nodded. In *Ivesiana* the individuals are either attacked outright, or they
carefully hide the meaningfulness of their feelings so they won't be. Love
in *Ivesiana* is revealed solely in terms of frustration: the beloved girl is
not even touched by her lover, and indeed she herself is never permitted
to touch the ground.

   And socially, *Ivesiana* is constantly irrupting with enemies. *Roma* is
just the opposite, everyone is friends. If Mr. Eglevsky at times seems a
little worldly and athletic, it may befit the lover; it would be interesting,
in this connection, to see Nicholas Magallanes (whose cavalier in *Nut-
cracker* was so nobly convincing) or Herbert Bliss (whose lover in *Scotch
Symphony* this season was so dramatically poetic) in the part to feel their
effect on the structure as a whole, since both maintain in most of their
performances a more organic relation to the corps than does Mr. Eglevsky
— though this is perhaps beside the point.

   At any rate, *Roma* seems a noble work, in terms of definition rather
than admiration. The definition comes from the 19th century, but we
have no more admirable term, unless it be honesty, and all Mr. Balanchine's
ballets have that.

[Balanchine's *Roma* was first performed at the City Center in New York
City on February 23, 1955, to the music of Georges Bizet, scenery and
costumes of Eugene Berman, and the lighting of Jean Rosenthal. Ed.]

RARE MODERN

Among contemporary painters there is a great distaste for academicism. But, judging by much recent poetry, this is not true of the poets. The latter do not feel that their art is contemporary, they feel that their loneliness is; for them, being academic is a way of being friendly with the other poets. In our decade and that previous, the motto of the Academy has been "We are all in the same fix together," and the two-fold solution proposed is doubly anti-poetic: the encouragement of a taste for technical facility which makes it easier for the poet to write while it makes it easier for the public to like what he writes. How many recent books resemble a "good design" show! Poet and public are being brought together by that famous American subject of communication, know-how. And everyone becomes friends at the wake of Art.

For a while this communication took place in the Green Room of the University after readings, but recently, as Mr. Horace Gregory points out in the current *Partisan Review,* it has begun to reach suburbia via booster stations, such as *The New Yorker.* But *The New Yorker* is not to blame, it was already in the air. Even more recently, poetry readings have been given for audiences which are neither primarily academic nor ultimately suburban; merely interested. In Boston, Chicago, New York, San Francisco and Seattle, to indicate a rough geographical outline, informal readings have met with lively, mixed responses, largely non-technological. And this is a good sign: isolated in reading, as in writing, the poet is in one fix and the audience in another. An isolation from the audience *by poetry* is a fairly gratifying situation, for inside each poet, I suspect, lurks a Garboesque desire. In the midst of this active isolation, the interests of other poets, of the University, of suburbia, of the Zeitgeist, become appropriately pale.

However, the critical apparatus of poetic technology is still with us and its subjects are far from few. Apart from the "soandso handles quatrains more adroitly than soandso" and the "esthetic machine of dazzling coherence and understatement" critiques, one may still be warned against certain poets who are beyond the academic concern for very odd reasons: we may be told that Hart Crane was over-ambitious, that William Carlos Williams does not "employ" clear, concise expression, or that Elizabeth Bishop is unachieved. This will seem, I hope, far-fetched; but all of us are prey to near-sightedness at one time or another. Even Mr. Gregory, who ignores Mr. Ashbery's first book because Mr. Auden mentions it in connection with Rimbaud. Since the other two poets under discussion are also outside the Academic-suburban-communications area, they are already isolated and the problem is how to see each, singly, and then, amidst all the humming, hear each, singly.

Mr. Kallman* is known to opera-lovers for his felicitous translations (*The Coronation of Poppea, Falstaff, The Abduction from the Seraglio*) and for his collaborations with W. H. Auden (Stravinsky's *The Rake's Progress,* an English version of *The Magic Flute*). Like a tenor who is vocally assured, he takes a strong line in interpreting his role in the dedicatory sonnet:

> . . . and so we swore
> We'd make a music other than what sounded
> In shots by which the migrant quail were hounded
> Or what, in mad-song, breathed behind the door.

The concentration and force he brings to each poetic occasion, while musical, has none of the spontaneity of the "sweet singer"; he sings very high and very low with equal assurance, and his ambition toward this broad range has made his tone strong, his notes true, with now and then a convincing awkwardness in the effort to be emotionally complete. He does not relax, he does not try to be attractive. His seriousness leads him into unpleasant truths even in the shorter lyrics, and he has the quickness of comprehension to transform them. Their inclusion gives his work emotional verisimiltude. His high is love:

> Oak, fern, ivy and pine:
> What they are, not the sound spoken,
> The words only as invocation
> Permitting me their presence again.
> The bus climbed from the narrow plain,
> From the palm-lined shore; on the mountain
> Were oak, fern, ivy and pine,
> A tang in the air. I was not alone,
> I was not alone. And later when
> We returned, under a sickle moon
> The blue broke in a fleece-white ribbon

* *Storm at Castelfranco* by Chester Kallman.

Along the beach. We came down
Through the mountain air, not a word spoken . . .

His low is spleen:

In all the world is there more
Of a cretin than my neighbor,
My neighbor who loves me? Far
Into the night when the mercy
Of God, like a lie
Without mercy, lies on the earth, I
Covet my neighbor; but when
The sun, like the Son of Man,
Brings peace with a sword, I am clean
To meet it directly . . .

And the intervening distances, the middle tones which make up the balance
of any composition but the most determinedly ecstatic, give evidence of
a remarkable quality he seems to have learned from music: the mastery of
the episode. His lyrics are not made up of short musical phrases usually,
but of stanzaic breaths of statement and counterstatement balanced by
contrapuntal elaboration, absorbing the individual line in its longer
phrasing, and ending with a resounding *stretto* or pathetically affirmative
tierce de Picardie:

Will

She, if I go, leaving doubt
To follow as the wind sings *"Truly follow,"* leaving
The dear discovery,
The fanciful triumph, will she
Lead as you wait, my mother, wait me still

In a seaward wind upon a new shore,
Kindly to judge, enlighten, to smile
Good-bye and turn as before?
As the sirens' plaint as I pass forgives the living
For life, as here and now
The bearing wind is true, the prow,
Cutting the beach, exults in winning style

Sheer above the mount; home there, as the long
Day hovers in the summer of love,
The food arrives, and the song
That shakes through the clacking birch is of arriving
Always, as everywhere
Recalls me, shall I be: O there,
There if I weep I shall have cause enough.

This full musical sentence, definite in meaning though not always
specific, appears as ardently in the poems of spleen as in the poems of
love, and is at its most fluent in the longer poems: "Atavisms," "Elegy,"
the title poem, and the splendidly intransigeant "Nightmare of a Cook."

Another distinguished first book, John Ashbery's *Some Trees,* appears
in the Yale Series of Younger Poets. In his graceful preface Mr. Auden
has explored one aspect of the poems, specifically their relation to the
dream-impulse in French Surrealism, so I shall pass on to other reflections,
pausing only to add that I find this quality in the work opposed to the
conscious elaboration of emotional response which ultimately became a
forced passionate tone in the American Surrealists. Mr. Ashbery writes
with a delightfully dry wit, using it discriminatingly to enhance a lyrical
mode which is predominantly tender. This tenderness knowingly dom-
inates the most unpersonal characteristics of modern life, as well as
those which are the conditions of its growth in the poet. He attempts
to look deeply into the actual matter of natural events, rather, it seems,
than risk an interpretation which might only be a comfortable means
of looking away. A suicide, for instance, feels she is performing a saintly
act of imitating nature, and says:

"I want to move

Figuratively, as waves caress
The thoughtless shore. You people I know

Will offer me every good thing
I do not want. But please remember

I died accepting them."

And sometimes nature tricks those who imitate her:

It is best to travel like a comet, with the others, though
          one does not see them.
How far that bridle flashed! "Hurry up, children!" The birds
          fly back, they say, "We were lying,
We do not want to fly away." But it is already too late. The
          children have vanished.

Everywhere in the poems there is the difficult attention to calling
things and events by their true qualities. He establishes a relation between
perception and articulateness which is non-rhetorical and specific; this
relation is consciously desired by the poet, beyond bitterness and fatigue,
and he even generously attributes it to others:

We see us as we truly behave:
From every corner comes a distinctive offering.
The train comes bearing joy;
The sparks it strikes illuminate the table,
Destiny guides the water-pilot, and it is destiny . . .

This is perhaps a day of general honesty
Without example in the world's history
Though the fumes are not of a singular authority
And indeed are dry as poverty.

How often honesty becomes general in these poems! and it is a con-
siderable technical achievement that the poems open outward to the
reader revealing a person other than the poet, whom we admire with the
poet for his courageous otherness: Colin in "Eclogue," the nun in "Illus-
tration," the poet as a child in "The Picture of Little J. A. in a Prospect
of Flowers," the solitary resident of the "Hotel Dauphin," "The Young
Son." They are all people who meet experience on the most articulate
lyrical terms and this gives their meetings an absolute value beyond their
quietly tragic disappointment, even as it is happening to "A Boy":

That night it rained on the boxcars, explaining
The thought of the pensive cabbage roses near the boxcars.
My boy. Isn't there something I asked you once?
What happened? It's also farther to the corner
Aboard the maple furniture. *He*

Couldn't lie. He'd tell 'em by their syntax.
But listen now in the flood.
They're throwing up behind the lines.
Dry fields of lightning rise to receive
The observer, the mincing flag. *An unendurable age.*

Things explain, nature reveals, and it is no aid to being.

In these few words I have perhaps overemphasized the poems of elegiac
content. There are amusing poems, too, sometimes with references to
other poets which are not quite parody, such as: "He" (Blaise Cendrars),
"The Thinnest Shadow" (Housman), "Canzone" (Auden), "The Instruction
Manual" (Whitman). Or perhaps I am misreading them, for each is brilliant
and touching in itself. I have left till last the mention of certain excellent
poems. It would be false to try to indicate their quality by a remark and
there is not space for exegeses, but I should at least single them out: "The
Grapevine," "Poem," "Album Leaf," "Pantoum," "The Orioles," "And You
Know," and "Answering a Question in the Mountains." Faultless music,
originality of perception – Mr. Ashbery has written the most beautiful
first book to appear in America since *Harmonium.*

I had recently been rereading Mr. Denby's first book, *In Public, In
Private,* a kind of "poet in New York" with its acute and painful sensibil-
ity, its vigorous ups and downs and stubborn tone. Since its appearance
in 1948, it seems an increasingly important book for the risks it takes in
successfully establishing a specifically American spoken diction which has
a classical firmness and clarity under his hand. He contributed then a
number of our very few fine sonnets and the remarkable city-poem,
"Elegy: The Streets," along with other, less perfect, but true, vital poems.

Mediterranean Cities is a handsome publication, printed in Italy and
adorned with photographs by Rudolph Burckhardt, the gifted artist and
film-maker. The new poems are sonnets on places and, as in Proust, the
artist's feelings become the sensibility of the places; *Mediterranean Cities*
follows a Proustian progression of sensation, reflection, awareness, sponta-
neous memory and apotheosis, a progression which proceeds from the
signal absorption in locale ("place names") and its accidental character-
istics to the emergence of the poet's being from his feelings in "the place."
The poet himself is eventually the place.

While the interior of the sequence, the book as a whole, is related to
Proust's method in my mind, another reference suggests itself. Unlike
the many poems-about-Europe-by-Americans we have had recently, the

"Fulbright poems," as someone recently described them, Mr. Denby's sonnets are in the great tradition of the Romantics, and particularly Shelley. With similar delicacy and opacity, and with a great deal more economy, he fixes the shifting moods, the sympathetic grasp of meaning in what the vulgar see only as picturesque, the pervading melancholy which overcomes the poet when he unites with the inanimate; this all reminds one of the English Romantic poets on the continent, and is reinforced by a cultural maturity like that of the Romantics (whatever one may think of their emotional status) which has seldom been achieved by an American poet in specific relation to the European past and his own present. But, being the work of a modern poet, Mr. Denby's sonnets do not rise to end in a burst of passionate identification, they light up from within with a kind of Mallarméan lucidity. They are obscure poems, eminently worth understanding, and I find these references helpful, though they may seem to leap about. One of Mallarmé's favorite poems, after all, was by Shelley.

Unless I am very much mistaken, the sequence of the poems (it is not called a sonnet sequence) is very important, and concerns itself with evaluations of art and life, historical and personal, in a serious lyrical manner which, being itself art, is also graceful. Sometimes the poet is isolated before the subject, the self evaluating the subject in traditional fashion:

Who watched Antinous in the yellow water
Here where swollen plains gully, Roman and brown
Built for fun, before a flat horizon scattered
Fancies, such advanced ones, that lie overthrown;
Urbanely they still leer, his voided surprises
Curved reflections, double half-lights, coigns of rest
Embarrassing as a rich man without admirers
Peculiar like a middle-aged man undressed;
Over the view's silent groundswell floats a field
Enskied by one eerie undeviating wall
Far to a door; pointing up his quietude
Watchful Hadrian exudes a sour smell;
The ratty smell of spite, his wit, his laughter
Who watched Antinous smile in yellow water

This, for the reader, is a sort of landscape-with-poet, and presently we find the picture changing: it is poet-in landscape; not the physical prospect, but the past of the place has begun to absorb him.

> Are you Russians the boys said seeing us strange
> Easy in grace by a poster with bicycles
> Soft voices in a Baroque and Byzantine slum
> Lemon pickers by swelling seas rainbow-fickle;
> On the height drizzle, and among thyme and mint
> A small shepherd, a large canvas umbrella
> Leaps away down the crumbled ruins, timid
> Where once they fought in moonlight, and Athens fell . . .

And this becomes not merely being in a foreign place, a stranger to its myriad times, but also to one's own history:

> Harbor, lost is the Greece when I was ten that
> Seduced me, god-like it shone; in a dark town, trembling
> Like a runaway boy on his first homeless night
> Ahead I rush in the fearful sweep of longing
> A dead longing that all day blurred here the lone
> Clear shapes which light was defining for a grown man

In a climactic moment the poet finds in himself the living sentence of a culture which may be dying, but is slow to die, is living for his sake, the ambiguous nature of temporality made clear by the timeless exertion of consciousness:

> She lifts from men dead into my passing life
> A beauty of doubt that is homeless and not brief

It seems to me that Mr. Denby in these sonnets has created something modern and intrinsic, sensitive and strong. Incidentally, he seems to have lifted William Carlos Williams' famous moratorium on the sonnet. . . . But to close:

> Now in New York Jacob wants to have my cat
> He goes to school, he behaves aggressively

He is three and a half, age makes us do that
And fifty years hence will he love Rome in place of me?
For with regret I leave the lovely world men made
Despite their bad character, their art is mild

Mr. Denby's own art has the classical gift for giving, in the present tense.

[*Poetry,* February 1957]

TO HOWARD KANOVITZ

For you, seeing is not an act. Whether abstract or figurative, your subject is the matter of velleity to which you offer time and chance, the accidental attention of a historian who comes upon an unknown fact or of an analyst who comes upon a hidden motivation, and does not pass immediately on. It is this "not letting it pass" which is the action of the work, for the process of enlarging attention commits you to major emotions: the red of ambition, the blue of despair. It is all in yourself. You do not rise to a subject, a subject is aroused by a whim. I suspect if you were to paint a landscape it would be a random sketch of one. But when you paint a random form it is liable to assume the proportions of a landscape: when you felt a chance phrase of music the painting became filled with smoke, instruments, the melancholy smell of stale whiskey and again, blue; or when you attended the minute interior workings of a red mass it became a mountainous image of joy achieved. You do not have the eager noise of external discovery, you have the poetic silence of the self.

[From the catalog for a show at the Tibor de Nagy Gallery, September-October 1956.]

GREGORY CORSO

Gregory Corso and the other two leaders of the so-called Beat and San-Francisco-Renaissance-Generation are Easterners who went to the West Coast with their various gifts like the Magi of old, following a star which was shortly thereafter to be followed by a lot of publicity, as of yore. Publication of their works, particularly that of Ginsberg and Kerouac, has led to a lot of guff being handed them as Beat Generation spokesmen rather than writers, just as certain abstract painters were made available to critical chastisement once the hostile critic got ahold of the proposed generic term Action Painting. A recent charge of their being "Know-Nothing Bohemians" by Norman Podhoretz in *PR* need not be gone into here, since the "control" advocated by Mr. Podhoretz is a notoriously poor substitute for inspiration, and at that from a young writer who is rapidly becoming the Herman Wouk of criticism. The vulgarity attributed to their work with alarming generality I find present only in the work of an older "generation," well established before they hit the Coast: Rexroth, Ferlinghetti and Patchen. The real poetic "École du Pacifique" is in excellent shape, claiming as it may the geographical presence of Gary Snyder, Philip Whalen, Mike McClure, Jack Spicer and others.

The critical approach usually leveled against the "Beat" is one of very little use to any reader, all confused as it is generally with reactions to James Dean, jazz, juvenile delinquency, dope, miscegenation, and so on. If this line of reasoning were followed, could a Republican millionaire buy a Courbet (maybe they'd give them away!) or an anti-Semite read Zola? The extraordinary beauties of Corso's poems, as of Ginsberg's, are not going to be revealed to petty-minded littérateurs who want their verse Georgian and their scandals Hollywoodian.

Corso's first book, *The Vestal Lady on Brattle,* was published in 1955 before he went West and, while uneven, already indicates the stance which later would establish him as one of our leading young poets:

> In California I sang
> my Eastern culture into a dying Mexican's ear
> that couldn't hear
> and he died with a smile on his face

> The bastard had three gold teeth
> an ounce of tea
> a pocketful of payote
> and a fourteen year old wife

The first stanza is lyrical and delicate in its perfection of ear and is character-
istic of the shorter lyrics which are one of his greatest skills, a perfection of
brevity which few contemporaries can rival, as witness the "For Bunny Lang":

> There in the greater light
> in the trembling urgency of the night
> I see a dead music
>   pursued by a dead listener.

or again:

> My hands are a city, a lyre
> And my hands are afire
> And my mother plays Corelli
>   while my hands burn

Corso is also the only poet who, to my taste, has adopted successfully the
rhythms and figures of speech of the jazz musician's world without em-
barrassment and with a light, musical certainty in its employment. While
the elegy to Bird Parker does not seem to me a good poem, others in *The
Vestal Lady* are notable, among them:

IN THE TUNNEL-BONE OF CAMBRIDGE

1
In spite of voices —
Cambridge and all its regions
Its horned churches with fawns' feet
Its white-haired young
        and ashfoot legions —
I decided to spend the night

But that hipster-tone of my vision agent
Decided to reconcile his sound with the sea
        leaving me flat

North of the Charles
                So now I'm stuck here —
                a subterranean
                lashed to a pinnacle

2
I don't know the better things that people know
All I know is the deserter condemned me to black —
He said: Gregory, here's two boxes of night
                one tube of moon
And twenty capsules of starlight, go an' have a ball —
He left and the creep took
                all my Gerry Mulligan records with him

3
But he didn't cut out right then
I saw him hopping
On Brattle street today —
                he's got a bum leg —
                on his way to the tunnel-bone
He made like he didn't see me
He was trying to play it cool

4
Wild in the station-bone
Strapped in a luggage vision-bone
                made sinister by old lessons of motion
The time-tablebone said: Black

Handcuffed to a minister
Released in a padded diesel
The brakeman punched my back: Destination, black

Out the window I could see my vision agent
                hopping along the platform
                swinging a burning-lantern-bone like mad
All aboard, he laughed, all aboard

Far into the tunnel-bone I put my ear to the ear
　　　of the minister — and I could hear
　　　the steel say to the steam
　　　and the steam to the roar: a black ahead
A black ahead a black and nothing more.

V. R. LANG: A MEMOIR

I first saw Bunny Lang 10 years ago at a cocktail party in a book store in Cambridge, Massachusetts. She was sitting in a corner sulking and biting her lower lip — long blonde hair, brown eyes, Roman-striped skirt. As if it were a movie, she was glamorous and aloof. The girl I was talking to said: "That's Bunny Lang. I'd like to give her a good slap."

We met a few weeks later and began a friendship which was unique — in my life, at least; perhaps not in hers, for she always kept certain areas of mystery intact. We had a fencing period: we sounded each other out for hours over beers, talking incessantly. We were both young poets and poetry was our major concern.

We both loved Rimbaud and Auden; she thought I loved Rimbaud too much, and I thought the same about Auden and her. She simply couldn't like Cocteau and couldn't bear *Ivan the Terrible.* "It's so black," she would say, "I don't believe a minute of it!" And we then began our "coffee talks" which were to go on for years, sometimes long distance. At 11 each morning we called each other and discussed everything we had thought of since we had parted the night before, including any dreams we may have had in the meantime. And once we were going to write a modern Coffee Cantata together, but never did.

She worked on her poems and plays in secrecy, withdrawn in the big room at the top of the old Boston house, looking out at the Charles River and ignoring her two noisy Siamese cats, which were almost always in heat. She would type her poems over and over, sometimes 40 times, sinking into them and understanding them. As for the theatre, she loved to sing, act, and dance, all of which she did with extraordinary charm and wit. Her first ideas for the theatre were on the charade or satire level; it was not until she began working on her first long play, *Fire Exit,* that her characteristic poetic process moved on stage, and in *Arcadia* it has found its starring role, a pastoral played in depth of feeling and solitude. A modern "Shepheards Calendar," the lovers rehearse for each other the seasons and the years, tarnished lovers seeking a justification for existence in their love. There on their island the City presses down upon them, initiating the failure of love, which is death.

Bunny's poems are full of the many things she did, the trips, the adventures, the stint with the Canadian WAC during the war, the literati in the *Chicago Review* days, the avant-garde in the Village, the circus on the stage, and through them all runs the stong line of her private world, the personal gaiety and suffering which relates her experiences and forms her existence. In *I Too Have Lived in Arcadia* appears the ultimate expression of her experience, and in these days of overnaturalism in the theatre, it is good to have a work for the theatre which is poetry, which articulately faces the hip compulsive with the pterodactyl and ponders both the survival of the fittest and the fitness of the survivor.

Perhaps we have become like cave creatures,
Who, being blind, can only the blind beget.
Sight is becoming useless. We are turning black. Well,
We will sweat now, like shuddering mountains
Struggling to grow in the millions of long time.
But squashed in the heart of us, surely there are footsteps
Of all the monsters who kept us alive.

In the summer of 1956, V. R. Lang died at the age of 32, the courage and fastidiousness of her life matched only by that of her work. And gradually that clear image of herself which is her work will be the sole image, a beautiful image, faithful to the original.

[Written for the *Village Voice* (October 23, 1957) on the occasion of the production of *I Too Have Lived in Arcadia* by the YM-YWHA. "A Personal Preface," dated 1961, was intended perhaps for *The Pitch,* a posthumous volume of V. R. Lang's poems and plays.]

A PERSONAL PREFACE

I am sitting here and cool sunlight, pretending to be warm, is coming through the window. Near me is a small color photograph of Bunny Lang, blonde, dark-eyed, ironically smiling, and in front of me a little toy tiger she once gave me, with a red ribbon around its waist. On the radio *Wozzeck* is playing, a work we often argued lovingly about (where Bunny didn't at first accept all the music, she was crazy about the heroine, Marie).

I also have a black dunce-cap, decorated with silver bells. She gave it to me to wear when I wrote. "It will keep you relaxed," she said, "free from distractions. It will keep away SPOOKS!" When Bunny was your friend, she was not only a dear friend, she was also the guardian of that friendship. And the guardian of so much else besides! of her own mysterious dreams, her strange insights, her sometimes savage honesty. You see this in the heroines of her plays who, like Marie, are beset but unyielding.

It is now five years since she died; it seems a moment, it seems it didn't happen at all. She is calling us long distance in these poems, telling us how it is with her, how bright things can be, how terrible things are. She was a wonderful person. She is one of our finest poets. We are so lucky to have something of her still!

FRANZ KLINE TALKING

FRANK O'HARA: Franz Kline's is one of the most outstanding achievements in contemporary painting. As a leader of the movement which is frequently called "American type painting" abroad and is described as abstract expressionism or action painting here, his work embodies those qualities of individuality, daring and grandeur which have made the movement a powerful influence. The painters of this movement, so totally different from each other in aspect, so totally without the look of a school, have given us as Americans an art which for the first time in our history we can love and emulate, aspire to and understand, without provincial digression or prejudice. The Europeanization of our sensibilities has at last been exorcized as if by magic, an event of some violence which Henry James would have hailed as eagerly as Walt Whitman and which allows us as a nation to exist internationally. We have something to offer and to give besides admiration on the one hand and refuge on the other.

Kline's role in this achievement has been a compelling one. His work does not represent an esthetic "stand" for or against a past or present style, nor has he sought the absolute of a pure esthetic statement. These personages which are at the same time noble structures (*Cardinal, Elizabeth, Siegfried*), these structures which are at once tragic personages *Wanamaker Block, Bridge, C & O*), seem both to express and to live by virtue of the American dream of power, that power which shuns domination and subjection and exists purely to inspire love.

Kline's studio is high-ceilinged and light and bare, with tall north windows facing on West 14th Street from the second floor. It is a floor through, and the south windows (French) give onto a terrace which is the roof of the store beneath (or is it a bar?). At the edge of this terrace, which has only two sun chairs and is bare like the studio, a little forest of trees-of-heaven partly hides a small tin building, apparently the rear of a 13th Street restaurant. Inside again, there are three or four painting walls of various sizes and early and recent paintings are stacked casually about. To see some of the paintings shown at the Egan Gallery in the late forties and early fifties is to take part in one of art's great dramas, the reaffirmation of value, a drama which has the added poignance of meeting again someone you once loved and who is more beautiful than ever. Near them are several recent works employing more color; side by side with the earlier works they state the inexorability of change in the environment of truly living forms:

"This is our life yesterday, this our life today." Kline is one of those lighthouses toward which Baudelaire directed our gaze: what is thrilling is that they are shining here, in our very time.

He is an ardent conversationalist but in his studio he is quiet. Everything is clear there, as it is at his exhibitions. We went to my place for the talk which follows.

FRANZ KLINE: That's Bill's isn't it? Terrific! You can always tell a de Kooning, even though this one doesn't look like earlier ones or later ones. It's not that style has a particular look, it just adds up. You become a stylist, I guess, but that's not it.

Somebody will say I have a black-and-white style, or a calligraphic style, but I never started out with that being consciously a style or attitude about painting. Sometimes you do have a definite idea about what you're doing – and at other times it all just seems to disappear. I don't feel mine is the most modern, contemporary, beyond-the-pale, *gone* kind of painting. But then, I don't have that kind of fuck-the-past attitude. I have very strong feelings about individual paintings and painters past and present.

Now, Bonnard at times seems styleless. Someone said of him that he had the rare ability to forget from one day to another what he had done. He added the next day's experience to it, like a child following a balloon. He painted the particular scene itself: in form, the woman can't quite get out of the bathtub. And he's a real colorist. The particular scene itself? Matisse wouldn't let that happen, he didn't let himself get too entranced with anything.

In Braque and Gris, they seemed to have an idea of the organization beforehand in their mind. With Bonnard, he is organizing in front of you. You can tell in Léger just when he discovered how to make it like an engine, as John Kane said, being a carpenter, a joiner. What's wrong with that? You see it in Barney Newman too, that he knows what a painting should be. He paints as he thinks *painting* should be, which is pretty heroic.

What with the drying and all, you can tell immediately pretty much whether a painting was done all at once or at different intervals. In one Picasso you can see it was all immediate, spontaneous, or in another that he came back the next day and put on the stroke that completed it. Sometimes you get one of those dark Ryders; it's the top one and it's all spontaneous and immediate, done all at once, and there are seven or eight others underneath it you can't tell about.

Now I'm not saying that doing it all at once implies an idea of the organization beforehand or that you like it when it's done all at once or that you like it when you've had the idea before you began. You instinctively like what you can't do. I like Fra Angelico. I used to try all the time to do those blue eyes that are really blue. Someone once told me to look at Ingres. I loved Daumier and Rembrandt at the time and I was bored when I looked at Ingres. Before long I began to like it. You go through the different phases of liking different guys who are not like you. You go to a museum looking for Titian and you wind up looking at someone else. But the way of working before Cézanne is hidden. Cézanne is like an analyst and he seems to be right there, you can see him painting the side of a nose with red. Even though he wanted to paint like Velasquez.

They painted the object that they looked *at*. They didn't fit out a studio and start painting without a subject. I find that I do both. Hokusai painted Fuji because it was there. He and others remembered it and drew from their imagination of how they had tried to paint it when it was in front of them. When he paints Fuji with a brush − birds, mist, snow, etc. − it's not the photographic eye but his mind has been brought to the utter simplification of it, and that doesn't bring it into symbolism. With Hokusai it was more like Toulouse-Lautrec drawing dancers and wanting to draw like Degas who wanted to draw like Ingres. It has something to do with wanting to see people dance. Or like Rembrandt going to see Hercules Seghers' landscapes.

Malevitch is interesting to me. Maybe because you are able to translate through his motion the endless wonder of what painting could be, without describing an eye or a breast. That would be looking at things romantically, which painters don't do. The thing has its own appeal outside of the white-on-white, this-on-that idea. With Mondrian, in a way you see that the condition is that he's a guy who solves his own problems illogically. He's done it with paint illogically to himself − which makes it logical to some other people. I was at the studio of one of these people one day and he said he was going to put red in one of the squares to improve it and what did I think? I said try it out and see if you like it, not if it improves it.

There's this comedian I know in the borscht circuit. They had a theater group and everything up there and my friend asked me to go there and teach painting. I told him I didn't have the money to get there and he said he'd send it to me. I got up there and talked with this comedian. He had studied with Raphael Soyer and painted, but he never could sell anything, so he took this job as a comedian and never got back to painting.

He loved Jackson Pollock and had such marvelous heart about it all that
he could never have been popular at either painting *or* comedy. He *cared*
so much. Somebody did an imitation of my drawing on a napkin, laughing,
six lines, and said, "That's all there is to it." My friend said, "That's why I
like it."

Then of course there are reviewers. I read reviews because they are a
facet of someone's mind which has been brought to bear on the work. Al-
though if someone's against it, they act as if the guy had spent his life
doing something worthless.

Someone can paint *not* from his own time, not even from himself. Then
the reviewer cannot like it, maybe. But just to review, like a shopper, I saw
one this, one that, good, awful, is terrible. Or he may be hopelessly unin-
terested in what it is anyway, but writes about it. I read Leonard Lyons in
the john the other day and he said every other country picked out the best
art for the Venice Biennale, but we didn't. Then someone in the govern-
ment went to Brussels and said painters should have to get a license for
buying brushes. Lyons went on to say he hoped that there will be a day
when abstractions are not supposed to be made for a child's playroom.

Criticism must come from those who are around it, who are not shocked
that someone should be doing it at all. It should be exciting, and in a way
that excitement comes from, in looking at it, that it's *not* that autumn
scene you love, it's *not* that portrait of your grandmother.

Which reminds me of Boston, for some reason. You know I studied there
for a while and once later I was up there for a show and met this Bostonian
who thought I looked pretty Bohemian. His definition of a Bohemian
artist was someone who could live where animals would die. He also talked
a lot about the 8th Street Club and said that Hans Hofmann and Clem
Greenberg run it, which is like Ruskin saying that Rowlandson and Daumier
used up enough copper to clad the British Navy and it's too bad they
didn't sink it. Why was he so upset about an artists' club in another city?
You get classified as a New York painter or poet automatically. They do it
in Boston or Philadelphia, you don't do it yourself.

Tomlin. In a way, they never did much about him and I think it's sad.
He didn't start an art school, but he had an influence — his statements
were very beautiful. When Pollock talked about painting he didn't usurp
anything that wasn't himself. He didn't want to change anything, he wasn't
using any outworn attitudes about it, he was always himself. He just
wanted to be in it because he loved it. The response in the person's mind
to that mysterious thing that has happened has nothing to do with who

did it first. Tomlin, however, did hear these voices and in reference to his early work and its relation to Braque, I like him for it. He was not an academician of cubism even then, he was an extremely personal and sensitive artist. If they want to talk about him, they say he was supposed to be Chopin. He didn't knock over any tables. Well, who's supposed to be Beethoven? Braque? I saw Tomlin's later work at the Arts Club in Chicago when he was abstract and it was the most exciting thing around – you look up who else was in the show.

If you're a painter, you're not alone. There's no way to be alone. You think and you care and you're with all the people who care, including the young people who don't know they do yet. Tomlin in his late paintings knew this. Jackson always knew it: that if you meant it enough when you did it, it will mean that much. It's like Caruso and Bjoerling. Bjoerling sounds like Caruso, but if you think of Caruso and McCormack you think of being in the world as you are. Bjoerling sounded like Caruso, but it turned out to be handsome. Bradley Tomlin didn't. Unless . . . Hell, if you look at all the painting in the world today it will probably all turn out to be handsome, I don't know.

The nature of anguish is translated into different forms. What has happened is that we're not through the analytical period of learning what motivates things. If you can figure out the motivation, it's supposed to be all right. But when things are "beside themselves" what matters is the care these things are given by someone. It's assumed that to read something requires an ability beyond that of a handwriting expert, but if someone throws something on a canvas it doesn't require any more care than if someone says, "I don't give a damn."

Like with Jackson: you don't paint the way someone, by observing your life, thinks you *have* to paint, you paint the way you have to in order to *give,* that's life itself, and someone will look and say it is the product of knowing, but it has nothing to do with knowing, it has to do with giving. The question about knowing will naturally be wrong. When you've finished giving, the look surprises you as well as anyone else.

Of course, this must be an American point of view. When Delacroix talks about the spirit, it must be French. It couldn't be Russian or Japanese. But writing his journals doesn't make him knowledgeable or practical. Delacroix was more interesting than that. That isn't the end in relation to his paintings. If it had been the end, people would have thought it interesting. Some people do think so.

Some painters talking about painting are like a lot of kids dancing at a prom. An hour later you're too shy to get out on the floor.

Hell, half the world wants to be like Thoreau at Walden worrying about the noise of traffic on the way to Boston; the other half use up their lives being part of that noise. I like the second half. Right?

To be right is the most terrific personal state that nobody is interested in.

[*Evergreen Review* II:6, Autumn 1958]

NORMAN BLUHM

> *"But who can re-create around us that immensity, that density of being which was really created for us and which once, though not from the gods, lapped around us on all sides?"* —René Char

We find everywhere in the works of the leading contemporary artists a preoccupation with spatial reality. It is not simply a quest for spatial enlightenment, but the longing to recreate that sense of space which we feel had once set free our dignity and candor, and is now only a half-doubtful memory. Despite the high level of ambition and execution witnessed in almost every country since the war, few artists can give to us that immensity and density which allows our spirits to elaborate and to founder, to leap and to fall back, with hope.

Among these few, Bluhm has a particular significance. His paintings — passionate, precise, impulsive, classical — embrace the elements of actuality as they are sensed rather than seen, and if there is reference to nature it is to those pure Empedoclean qualities which we had thought lost: earth, fire, water, air. The grandeur of this conception is apparent. Its pertinence will continue to reverberate and to enlighten us as our sensibilities grow clearer in its luminosity and definition.

[Written for the catalog of a show at the Galleria del Naviglio, Milan, 1959]

LARRY RIVERS: *The Next to Last Confederate Soldier*

American painting is in such a splendid state of confusion that it is a joy to contemplate. Would that poetry were in the same state! And perhaps it's approaching it, for the reasons for loving a poem by Allen Ginsberg are the same reasons for loving a poem by John Ashbery, or by Kenneth Koch, or by Gregory Corso, just as the reasons for loving a painting by Franz Kline are the same for one by Michael Goldberg: they are all distinct, individual responses to distinct, individual meaningfulness — which varies so widely in scope, in drama, in contact, that the engaged person is reeling *at last* from contact with his own life, contact which the rest of society tries to teach him to back away from like a sick leopard who doesn't know which trainer has his best interests at heart.

In this pocket-abyss where one doesn't know where one is at, where a large red painting may be a Grace Hartigan or a howitzer, where one has nightmares about not knowing what one is looking at, the only thing you have to hold onto is your own natural savagery, and your ability to recognize your own *natural* savagery has been given to you by this art which in turn is the cause of your anxiety about not being able to recognize anything but yourself. And that is the last thing one wishes to recognize. Most of us would much prefer to be Zen neophytes identifying herbs.

Much has been said about the work of Jasper Johns recently — but how anyone can find his big white flag painting enigmatic is beyond me, a painting which forces a recognition in me to where I am at the brink of hysterical tears when my movie-fed head is inclined toward the *Raft of the Medusa*. ("Boys! don't leave me behind!" — Palinurus.) The same thing occurs with De Kooning's *Suburb in Havana*. Why should it have this overpowering effect when we have the House of Seagram in front of us?

This is the concern of art in our time, supplying, for better or worse, something which we undoubtedly deserve, although its name is not so simply sociological as "identity." It might be more clearly and less lazily called risk. It is comfortable to ask yourself to risk, but it is more serious when the request comes from outside yourself and not from another person.

A lot of blank, gorgeous art has proceeded from the awareness that modern art has tended to be centered on the recognition of subject and object as being the same. And this *is* an extraordinary phenomenon from the historical point of view: that the subject and object have suddenly again become unified, as in pre-Greek sculpture and a very few other periods, equally phenomenal and very far away. But this beautiful blank art (and I don't mean Newman or Rothko), a by-product, merely expresses the canniness of the artist, it holds up a mirror of color and/or impasto to the viewer who cannot participate in the recognition because it is the artist recognizing the cultural audience. These effete Barbizon pictures are merely a clue to seeing a Kline.

Where does Rivers figure in all this? He appears at the intersection of the great forced-recognition art of our time and of that of the mirror-recognition of this art. He shifts and feints like Sugar Ray Robinson, if you double he redoubles like George Rapée. He is an enigma, and he is fascinating. While he lends identity to his audience, he refuses to adopt that identity for the comfort of the audience. His best works are often the least consequential. Rivers fights a long, devious, and obscure fight and dares you to identify the combatants. The elemental *presence* of art is in his work. Apparently the fact that *The Next to Last Confederate Soldier* is a corny subject led him to expend on it an austerity of technical means which is beyond what he had discovered in himself before. On the other hand, the *Soldier* is not the subject of this painting, but the occasion of its appearance, for Rivers' work belongs to that art which is spoken of as being "other."

The blueness, the redness of the flag (flags everywhere! – "we are indeed dying!"), the umber-ochre face of barely surviving heroes, is lost in the linear acuity and tenderness, and the cool, powerful masses of oncoming silence, all in a scale and of a grandeur which is refusing the simple identification of an image while being as simple as technical means can be. Rivers is a lyrical painter putting historical subject-matter through its paces (as he did earlier in *George Washington Crossing the Delaware,* another sporadic foray into the recherché), and the painting itself comes out on top.

One of the sculptures I have most admired in the last few years, Rivers' *Kabuki in a Rectangle*, was identified by the painter Matsumi Kanemitsu. Without the help of a *Life* magazine photograph the present *Confederate Soldier* would go unidentified. Rivers is not only refusing to recognize the audience, he is denying the audience the opportunity to recognize him. Not since Arshile Gorky has there been so intransigent a stand on identity. *The Soldier's* fluctuation between figurative absence and abstract presence comes from an adamant attachment to substance, which is its source of energy. That is all, no identity. In his work Rivers playing out, at whatever cost to himself, the drama of our lack.

[From *School of New York: Some Younger Artists,* edited by B.H. Friedman, Grove Press, 1959.]

AMERICAN ART AND NON-AMERICAN ART

I am sure that anything I have to say on this subject will bring down upon me the terrifying disproofs of Kaldis, but nothing ventured, nothing gained, just so long as he keeps speaking to me. So far as I can see lately, what we mean by American art is, with a few exceptions such as Giacometti, Wols and Riopelle, simply avant-garde art. It is still alive, it is part of our lives (not nationally – personally), it can be experienced without necessarily being understood completely, it can move us and remain a mystery. We are not yet art-trained to appreciate it (though we may be life-trained to). Little of the European art of recent years affects me in this way, excepting in addition to the above Canogar, Saura, perhaps Jorn. I don't think this is because I am an American myself, though it may be.

It is not illogical if American art turns out to be the major avant-garde art of the period. The American is in quite a different position from the artist in any of the great art-producing countries of Europe. I don't know about Japan. The only force he can bring to bear on society, the only way he can be heard, is in (not through) his work. No American committee of writers is going to get anyone out of jail. Few Americans consider a great artist a source of national pride, and certainly the government is not going to reward him. This is all a great advantage which has been put to use.

Europeans always talk about commitment in the singular, but they always seem to have two: esthetic and political. The American artist is much more likely to have put all his eggs in one basket. His metaphysical quality, which is often denied but for lack of a better word I shall use, is the result. The Spanish Pavilion at the last Venice Biennale probably achieved its quality because of a somewhat similar circumstance, culturally. It is no accident that so many of the brightest lights of the École de Paris were expatriates who had little or no means of expressing their social potency beyond their own work.

Europeans often find contemporary American art violent. I don't, but violence is the atmosphere in which much of it is created and which makes its commitment extreme and serious. New York is one of the most violent cities in the world and its pace is hectic. What can survive must have had some quality, what can be done under all the different pressures of circumstance must have meant something to the artist who managed to get it done. There is no velleity in the work of Pollock, de Kooning, Kline, Smith, Rothko, Newman, Still, et al., and that is what they have in common, that is all they have in common. This is true of several younger artists, too. This urgency in the art, and our sense of it, may well keep us from seeing non-American art truly. But it is a necessary risk for us, it is nothing compared to the risk of the artist which must make its own demands upon the rest of us.

Too, there is more sheer ugliness in America than you can shake a stick at. And it is the characteristic of the avant-garde to absorb and transform disparate qualities not normally associated with art, for the artist to take within him the violence and evil of his times and come out with something. A good example of the process is Gregory Corso's superb and praiseful poem *Bomb*. In this way society can bear and understand and finally appreciate the qualities of alien and even dangerous things. I am not saying that this is the purpose of art, but without these fiercenesses the art is different. There is more for the artist to do here, and I believe more is being done, than anywhere else in the world at present. The State Department wouldn't be so upset about satellites if it knew more about art, which will after all stay "up" longer than any of the projects planned by scientists to date. If any of us do get into the future, it will not be by means of a lot of spheres and tank suits.

If any of what I am saying is true, if there really is such a thing as American painting, I think it can only be because for the first time in our history an art is appearing which is aware of the rest of the world in a non-imitative way. And the more naked we get, the more clearly we will be seen to be ourselves. Why should we be ashamed? The French aren't ashamed of being French.

[In its Winter-Spring issue of 1959, *It Is* published "Six Opinions on Abstract Art in Other Countries" by Frank O'Hara, Thomas B. Hess, Paul Jenkins, Milton Resnick, William Ronald and Irving Sandler. We follow FOH's original ms here. Ed.]

ABOUT ZHIVAGO AND HIS POEMS

We are used to the old saw that poets cannot write great novels or indeed any novels. The adherents of this cliché, hoping to perpetuate a mystery-distinction between two kinds of writing, are cheered on by the novelists who hate "poetic" novels and the poets who hate "prosaic" poems. Virginia Woolf gets hers from one quarter and William Carlos Williams gets his from the other. The argument is usually bolstered by phrases like "Joyce *turned to* prose," which would have been an amusing scene, but never occurred. For what poetry gave to Joyce, as to Pasternak, is what painting gave to Proust: the belief that high art has a communicability far superior in scope and strength to any other form of human endeavor. The Nobel Prize committee was correct in making the award include Pasternak's poetry as well as the novel. To admirers of his poetry *Doctor Zhivago* is the epic expression of many of the themes first found in individual lyrics and short stories; the present epic form is the poet's response to the demand of his time for its proper expression.

With one prose masterpiece behind him, *Safe Conduct* (1931), Pasternak insists in *Doctor Zhivago* on identifying poetry with truth to the supreme extent: in no other work of modern literature do we wait for the final revelation of meaning to occur in the hero's posthumous book of poems. The political ramifications of the novel's publication have thrust the poet (author *and* hero) into dramatic relief for a vast international public and established the efficacy of the poet's stance in realms far beyond personal lyricism. The clamor over *Doctor Zhivago* has been denounced by various literary figures as damaging to Pasternak personally, but let there be no mistake about this clamor: it comes not from anything Pasternak has said in the press, nor from the phrasing of the Nobel Prize citation, nor from Western or Soviet political commentaries on the novel's content, it comes from the nature of the work itself. Of the critics only Edmund Wilson has seen this quality in its proper perspective. Pasternak has written a revolutionary and prophetic work which judges contemporary society outside as well as within the Iron Curtain. And if Pasternak is saying that the 1917 Revolution failed, he must feel that the West never even made an attempt. Far from being a traitorous work, *Doctor Zhivago* is a poem on the nobility of the Soviet failure to reconstruct society *in human terms,* and it is not without hope. The two disillusioning heroes of *Safe Conduct,* Scriabin and Mayakovsky, give way to the triumphant hero of *Doctor Zhivago*.

It is plain that this hero must be an artist; to Pasternak the artist is the last repository of individual conscience, and in his terms conscience is individual perception of life. This is not at all a counterrevolutionary attitude based on an intellectual-aristocratic system. It has not to do with a predilection for "culture." The lesson comes from life. Zhivago himself becomes a doctor, but he finds that his usefulness to society is everywhere stymied, that his social efficacy is incomplete and does not contribute to his understanding of his own predicament. To be a twentieth-century hero Zhivago must leave for subsequent generations a living testament. It does not suffice that he "live in the hearts of his countrymen" by remembered deeds alone. It is a question of articulation: the epic events of Doctor Zhivago demand from their participants articulate perception or mute surrender. Pasternak's epic is not the glorification of the plight of the individual, but of the accomplishment of the individual in the face of almost insuperable sufferings which are personal and emotionally real, never melodramatic and official. And it is the poet's duty to accomplish this articulation.

Everywhere in the work of Pasternak published in English, we saw this meaning growing. It is a world very like that of Joyce's characters as we meet them in *Dubliners* and *The Portrait of the Artist as a Young Man* and find them later older, clearer, changed, in *Ulysses* and *Finnegans Wake*. Obviously the young Larisa Feodorovna bears this kind of resemblance to the adolescent Zhenia Luvers of the early story (mistakenly printed as two distinct stories under separate titles by New Directions); several scenes in "Aerial Ways" anticipate events in the novel, and indeed Pasternak draws attention to this aspect of his writing in the opening passages of "A Tale" (called "The Last Summer" in English). It is the writer of the "Letters to Tula" who bears the strongest resemblance to Zhivago himself: "Everything that happens happens from the nature of the place. This is an event on the *territory of conscience,* it occurs on her own ore-bearing regions. There will be no 'poet.' " In this passage Pasternak reveals early (1918) his belief that the poet must first be a person, that his writings make him a poet, not his acting the role. I cannot agree with Elsa Triolet when she recently attacked Pasternak for having betrayed Mayakovsky in writing *Doctor Zhivago*. On the contrary, the principles which were later to seduce Mayakovsky had been exposed in "Letters to Tula" already:

. . . I swear to you that the faith of my heart is greater than ever it was, the time will come — no, let me tell you about that later. Tear me to pieces, tear me to pieces, night, burn to ashes, burn, burn brilliantly, luminously, the forgotten, the angry, the fiery word "Conscience"! Burn maddening, petrol-bearing tongue of the flame . . .

This way of regarding life has come into being and now there is no place on earth where a man can warm his soul with the fire of shame: shame is everywhere watered down and cannot burn. Falsehood and dissipation. Thus for thirty years all who are singular live and drench their shame, old and young, and already it has spread through the whole world, among the unknown . . .

The poet, henceforward inscribing this word, until it is purged with fire, in inverted commas, the "poet" observes himself in the unseemly behavior of actors, in the disgraceful spectacle which accuses his comrades and his generation. Perhaps he is only playing with the idea. No. They confirm him in the belief that his identity is in no way chimerical . . .

This passage is like a rehearsal of the talks Zhivago has with his uncle when they discuss principles. That it also bears on Pasternak's relationship with Mayakovsky is witnessed by the following passage from *Safe Conduct*:

But a whole conception of life lay concealed under the Romantic manner which I was to deny myself from henceforth. This was the conception of life as the life of the poet. It had come down to us from the Romantics, principally the Germans.

This conception had influenced Blok but only during a short period. It was incapable of satisfying him in the form in which it came naturally to him. He could either heighten it or abandon it altogether. He abandoned the conception. Mayakovsky and Esenin heightened it.

In the poet who imagines himself the measure of life and pays for this with his life, the Romantic conception manifests itself brilliantly and irrefutably in his symbolism, that is in everything which touches upon Orphism and Christianity imaginatively. In this sense something inscrutable was incarnate both in the life of Mayakovsky and in the fate of Esenin, which defies all epithets, demanding self-destruction and passing into myth.

But outside the legend, the Romantic scheme is false. The poet who is its foundation, is inconceivable without the nonpoets who must bring him into relief, because this poet is not a living personality absorbed in the study of moral knowledge, but a visual-biographical "emblem," demanding a background to make his contours visible. In contradistinction to the Passion plays which needed a Heaven if they were to be heard, this drama needs the evil of mediocrity in order to be seen, just as Romanticism always needs philistinism and with the disappearance of the petty bourgeoisie loses half its poetical content.

What then, after rejecting the concept of the Romantic "pose" in relation to his own life and art, does Pasternak's position become? He had already moved towards this decision in the poems written previous to 1917 and in a later volume he chooses the title from a poem, "My Sister Life." This expresses very clearly his position: the poet and life herself walk hand in hand. Life is not a landscape before which the poet postures, but the very condition of his inspiration in a deeply personal way: "My Sister, life, is in flood today . . . " This is not the nineteenth-century Romantic identification, but a recognition. In the later work Zhivago says to the dying Anna Ivanovna:

. . . But all the time, life, one, immense, identical throughout its innumerable combinations and transformations, fills the universe and is continually reborn. You are anxious about whether you will rise from the dead or not, but you rose from the dead when you were born and you didn't notice it . . .

So what will happen to your consciousness? *Your* consciousness, yours, not anyone else's. Well, what are you? There's the point. Let's try to find out. What is it about you that you have always known as yourself? What are you conscious of in yourself? Your kidneys? Your liver? Your blood vessels? No. However far back you go in your memory, it is always in some external, active manifestation of yourself that you come across your identity — in the work of your hands, in your family, in other people. And now listen carefully. You in others — this is your soul. This is what you are. This is what your consciousness has breathed and lived on and enjoyed throughout your life — your soul, your immortality, your life in others. And what now? You have always been in others and you will remain in others. And what does it matter to you if later on that is called your memory? This will be you — the you that enters the future and becomes a part of it . . .

There is every reason to believe that Pasternak's recognition of self was accompanied by great pain. He adored Mayakovsky at the time and indeed was forced to this decision of self by Mayakovsky's presence in that time, ". . . because poetry as I understand it flows through history and in collaboration with real life." Mayakovsky made a fatal error and became a tragic hero. Like Strelnikov in the novel, he succumbed to a belief in the self-created rhetoric of his own dynamic function in society. That society needed him and benefited from this rhetoric is obvious. But both he and the character in *Doctor Zhivago* ended in suicide when their usefulness in this function came to an end, and while their response to social demand seems shortsighted to Pasternak, he also condemned society for the temptation:

> The great Soviet gives to the highest passions
> In these brave days each one its rightful place,
> Yet vainly leaves one vacant for the poet.
> When that's not empty, look for danger's face.

The chair of poetry must remain empty, for poetry does not collaborate with society, but with life. Soviet society is not alone in seducing the poet to deliver temporary half-truths which will shortly be cast aside for the excitement of a new celebration of nonlife. The danger is that life does not allow any substitute for love.

It is not surprising then that this sense of poetry and its intimate connection with his relationship to life is one of the strongest elements in Zhivago's nature. It makes of Zhivago one of the most original heroes in Western literature, a man who cannot be interpreted by nineteenth-century standards, which I suspect Lionel Abel attempts to do when he says, writing in *Dissent,* ". . . how can he not have understood that in yielding to the impulse to write of his beloved immediately after his loss of her, he was taking a practical attitude toward his grief, trying to get something out of it, literature, maybe even glory?" What Mr. Abel misses finding here is the grief-expression of the romantic hero, which had been eschewed by Pasternak himself in an early poem which fits oddly well into the present scene of loss:

> . . . O miraculous obit, beckon, beckon! You may
> Well be astonished. For — look — you are free.

I do not hold you. Go, yes, go elsewhere,
Do good. *Werther* cannot be written again,
And in our time death's odor is in the air;
To open a window is to open a vein.

Far from shallow or opportunistic in his grief (being left alone in the Urals
with the wolves closing in would hardly raise hopes for literary fame),
Zhivago weeps, drinks vodka, scribbles poems and notes, is subject to
hallucinations, and begins the decline which will end in his death. But at
this crucial period of his life in which he unexpectedly suffers the ultimate
loss, that of Larisa Feodorovna, the period in which he had hoped to ac-
complish his poetic testament, his creativity does not desert him. We must
remember that the events of the post-revolution period have robbed him
of the time to think, the time to write. He saves his sanity by crowding
the writing and the speculations of a lifetime into these days of isolation,
coming to conclusions about certain events, and thus approaching once
again, after this interval of grief, his "sister, life":

. . . Mourning for Lara, he also mourned that distant summer in Meliu-
zeievo when the revolution had been a god come down to earth from
heaven, the god of the summer when everyone had gone crazy in his
own way, and when everyone's life had existed in its own right, and
not as an illustration for a thesis in support of the rightness of a supe-
rior policy.

As he scribbled his odds and ends, he made a note reaffirming his
belief that art always serves beauty, and beauty is delight in form,
and form is the key to organic life, since no living thing can exist
without it, so that every work of art, including tragedy, expresses
the joy of existence. And his own ideas and notes also brought him
joy, a tragic joy, a joy full of tears that exhausted him and made his
head ache.

He decides to forego the virtual suicide of his retreat in the snowy wil-
derness, in the abandoned house which has offered him, for the first time
since he was a student, the solitude for his poetry, and to return to Mos-
cow. The inverted commas have been purged from the word poet. And
unlike Chekhov's *Three Sisters* he does reach Moscow. And there he has
a tangible reality even after his death, as recognized by his two childhood
friends as they read at dusk the posthumous poems which Zhivago's mys-

teriously angelic half brother Evgraf has collected:

> . . . And Moscow, right below them and stretching into the dis-
> tance, the author's native city, in which he had spent half his life —
> Moscow now struck them not as the stage of the events connected
> with him but as the main protagonist of a long story, the end of
> which they had reached that evening, book in hand.
>
> Although victory had not brought the relief and freedom that
> were expected at the end of the war, nevertheless the portents of
> freedom filled the air throughout the postwar period, and they
> alone defined its historical significance.
>
> To the two old friends, as they sat by the window, it seemed
> that this freedom of the soul was already there, as if that very
> evening the future had tangibly moved into the streets below them,
> that they themselves had entered it and were now part of it . . .
>
> And the book they held seemed to confirm and encourage this
> feeling.

This is Zhivago's triumph over the terrible vicissitudes of love and cir-
cumstance which we have witnessed, the "active manifestation" of
himself — his soul, his immortality, his life in others.

Though the greatness of scale in *Doctor Zhivago* bears a resemblance to
Tolstoy's achievement, this is not a massively documented and described
war-novel like those we have had from Americans, French and Russian neo-
Tolstoyans, where the scheme is that of nineteenth-century prototypes
swamped by the events of their time. On the contrary, one of the great
beauties of Pasternak's technique is that of portraying events through the
consciousness of principal and minor characters. In this he resembles Joyce
and Proust; often we hear of an event from a character *after* it has changed
him, so that we apprehend both the event and its consequences simultane-
ously. The intimacy which this technique lends to the epic structure, par-
ticularly when the character is relatively unknown to us, and the discretion
with which it is handled, reminds one of two other works of perfect scale,
Lermontov's *A Hero of Our Times* and Flaubert's *A Sentimental Education*.

Nowhere in the novel is this method more rewarding than in the presen-
tation of the hero, and here it is varied beyond what I have described. Of
Yurii Andreievich Zhivago we know a great deal as we progress through the
novel. We not only know his feelings and his response to and attempted
evaluation of events. but also his longings. We even know what he considers

the most important elements in his life and how he intends to evaluate
them in his work. But here Pasternak's devastating distrust of the plane
of action in human affairs becomes clearest and makes its strongest
point. In the post-epilogue book of poems we find that Zhivago has not
written the poems he wanted to, nor the poems we expected (except for
the one on St. George); in the course of creating the poems he has be-
come not the mirror of the life we know, but the instrument of its per-
ceptions, hitherto veiled. This is the major expression of a meaning
which Pasternak has implied often in the novel proper. The human in-
dividual is the subject of historical events, not vice versa; he is the reposi-
tory of life's force. And while he may suffer, may be rendered helpless,
may be killed, if he has the perceptiveness to realize this he knows that
events require his participation to occur. In this context we find another
revolutionary reinterpretation of the human condition: Strelnikov, the
"active" Red Army Commissar, is rendered passive by his blind espousal
of principles whose needful occasion has passed; Zhivago, passively with-
drawn from action which his conscience cannot sanction, finds the art
for which an occasion will continue to exist. This qualitative distinction
between two kinds of significance is as foreign to our own society as it
is to that of the U.S.S.R.

The poems with which the novel culminates are truly Zhivago's own,
not Pasternak's. They deliver us a total image of the hero's life which is
incremented by details of that life from the prose section. While we rec-
ognize the occasions of many, we find their expression different from
what we, or Zhivago, expected. As an indication of how different they
are from Pasternak's own poems, we need only compare two poems on
a similar theme, Pasternak's lyric "If only when I made my début" and
Zhivago's "Hamlet." In the one, Pasternak deals with one of his central
themes which is mentioned above in relation to Mayakovsky. The poem
is full of the tragedy of human involvement, but in a pure, nonsymbolic
manner: it is the role taking over the actor, of course, but it is also the
word consuming the poet, the drama of the meaning, which the poet has
found through the act of creating this meaning, transporting him to an
area of realization beyond his power, where he has been joined to the
mortal presence of life:

> A line that feeling sternly dictates
> Sends on the stage a slave, and, faith,

> It is good-bye to art forever
> Then, then things smack of soil and Fate.

How different is Zhivago's poem on this theme. Not only does he assume a "masque," that of Hamlet, but before we are through the second stanza he has made the symbolic connection of Hamlet with the Hebraic-Christian myth of father-and-son positive by reference to Christ in the Garden of Olives. The poem ends on a reference to Zhivago's own physical circumstance, a personal note that has saved many a Symbolist poem:

> I stand alone. All else is swamped in Pharisaism.
> To live life to the end is not a childish task.

Because of the novel, we cannot resist the idea that this poem was written in the snowy forests of Varykino after Lara's departure, where Zhivago endures his agonizing "vigil" and decides to forego suicide and to return to Moscow.

The Christian poems are extraordinary achievements as poems, and also reveal how complicated the structure of the novel is. In reading them we realize for the first time how enormously influential on Zhivago was the interpretation of Christ's significance by a minor character who was speaking to Lara and overheard by him from the next room. It becomes clear that Zhivago's Christianity is no hieratic discipline, but a recognition of social change: " . . . you have a girl — an everyday figure who would have gone unnoticed in the ancient world — quietly, secretly bringing forth a child . . .

"Something in the world had changed. Rome was at an end. The reign of numbers was at an end. The duty, imposed by armed force, to live unanimously as a people, as a whole nation, was abolished . . . Individual life became the life story of God . . ." For those who have interpreted *Doctor Zhivago* with some smugness as a return to Christianity as the Western World knows it, it should be pointed out that this historical interpretation bears roughly the same analogy to Protestantism and Catholicism as they are practiced that Marxism does to Capitalism. It is not only based on historical distinctions, but "faith" is further set aside by the distinctions made in the poems between human life and nature, and the ambiguities of this relationship as they affect the Christ legend. When the fig tree is consumed to ashes in "Miracle," Zhivago writes:

If at that point but a moment of free choice had been granted
To the leaves, the branches, to the trunk and roots
The laws of nature might have contrived to intervene.

And in "Holy Week" our dependency on nature becomes the rival of God:

And when the midnight comes
All creatures and all flesh will fall silent
On hearing spring put forth its rumor
That just as soon as there is better weather
Death itself can be overcome
Through the power of the Resurrection.

It is not difficult to ascertain that for Pasternak the interdependency of
man and nature is far from theological. It is in these clarifications of feelings
and thoughts, in these poems, that Zhivago becomes a true hero. Here we
find his inner response to his wife's moving letter from exile which also
contains his reasons for not joining her outside Russia ("Dawn"), in other
poems his ambivalences and his social nobility. In the most revealing of
all, the love poems to Lara (including the superb "Autumn," "Parting,"
"Encounter" and "Magdalene"), we find the intensity which had so moved
her and which Zhivago himself reveals nowhere else except in the secrecy
of their own intimate hours. Her greatness in responding to this love
becomes even more moving in retrospect than it was when one first read
her thoughts at his bier, one of the greatest scenes in literature:

. . . Oh, what a love it was, utterly free, unique, like nothing else on
earth! Their thoughts were like other people's songs.
    They loved each other, not driven by necessity, by the "blaze of
passion" often falsely ascribed to love. They loved each other because
everything around them willed it, the trees and the clouds and the
sky over their heads and the earth under their feet. Perhaps their sur-
rounding world, the strangers they met in the street, the wide expanses
they saw on their walks, the rooms in which they lived or met, took
more delight in their love than they themselves did.

And the posthumous response to her love is on as grand a scale:

You are the blessing in a stride toward perdition,
When living sickens more than sickness does itself;
The root of beauty is audacity,
And that is what draws us to each other

It is this inevitability which makes *Doctor Zhivago* great, as if we, not Pasternak, had willed it. And if love lives at all in the cheap tempestuousness of our time, I think it can only be in the unrelenting honesty with which we face animate nature and inanimate things and the cruelty of our kind, and perceive and articulate and, like Zhivago, choose love above all else.

[*Evergreen Review* II:7, Winter 1959]

PERSONISM: A MANIFESTO

Everything is in the poems, but at the risk of sounding like the poor wealthy man's Allen Ginsberg I will write to you because I just heard that one of my fellow poets thinks that a poem of mine that can't be got at one reading is because I was confused too. Now, come on. I don't believe in god, so I don't have to make elaborately sounded structures. I hate Vachel Lindsay, always have, I don't even like rhythm, assonance, all that stuff. You just go on your nerve. If someone's chasing you down the street with a knife you just run, you don't turn around and shout, "Give it up! I was a track star for Mineola Prep."

That's for the writing poems part. As for their reception, suppose you're in love and someone's mistreating (*mal aimé*) you, you don't say, "Hey, you can't hurt me this way, I care!" you just let all the different bodies fall where they may, and they always do may after a few months. But that's not why you fell in love in the first place, just to hang onto life, so you have to take your chances and try to avoid being logical. Pain always produces logic, which is very bad for you.

I'm not saying that I don't have practically the most lofty ideas of anyone writing today, but what difference does that make? they're just ideas. The only good thing about it is that when I get lofty enough I've stopped thinking and that's when refreshment arrives.

But how can you really care if anybody gets it, or gets what it means, or if it improves them. Improves them for what? for death? Why hurry them along? Too many poets act like a middle-aged mother trying to get her kids to eat too much cooked meat, and potatoes with drippings (tears). I don't give a damn whether they eat or not. Forced feeding leads to excessive thinness (effete). Nobody should experience anything they don't need to, if they don't need poetry bully for them, I like the movies too. And after all, only Whitman and Crane and Williams, of the American poets, are better than the movies. As for measure and other technical apparatus, that's just common sense: if you're going to buy a pair of pants you want them to be tight enough so everyone will want to go to bed with you.There's nothing metaphysical about it. Unless, of course, you flatter yourself into thinking that what you're experiencing is "yearning."

Abstraction in poetry, which Allen recently commented on in *It Is,* is intriguing. I think it appears mostly in the minute particulars where decision is necessary. Abstraction (in poetry, not in painting) involves personal removal by the poet. For instance, the decision involved in the choice between "the nostalgia *of* the infinite" and "the nostalgia *for* the infinite" defines an attitude towards degree of abstraction. The nostalgia *of* the infinite representing the greater degree of abstraction, removal, and negative capability (as in Keats and Mallarmé). Personism, a movement which I recently founded and which nobody knows about, interests me a great deal, being so totally opposed to this kind of abstract removal that it is verging on a true abstraction for the first time, really, in the history of poetry. Personism is to Wallace Stevens what *la poésie pure* was to Béranger. Personism has nothing to do with philosophy, it's all art. It does not have to do with personality or intimacy, far from it! But to give you a vague idea, one of its minimal aspects is to address itself to one person (other than the poet himself), thus evoking overtones of love without destroying love's life-giving vulgarity, and sustaining the poet's feelings towards the poem while preventing love from distracting him into feeling about the person. That's part of Personism. It was founded by me after lunch with LeRoi Jones on August 27, 1959, a day in which I was in love with someone (not Roi, by the way, a blond). I went back to work and wrote a poem for this person. While I was writing it I was realizing that if I wanted to I could use the telephone instead of writing the poem, and so Personism was born. It's a very exciting movement which will undoubtedly have lots of adherents. It puts the poem squarely between the poet and the person, Lucky Pierre style, and the poem is correspondingly gratified. The poem is at last between two persons instead of two pages. In all modesty, I confess that it may be the death of literature as we know it. While I have certain regrets, I am still glad I got there before Alain Robbe-Grillet did. Poetry being quicker and surer than prose, it is only just that poetry finish literature off. For a time people thought that Artaud was going to accomplish this, but actually, for all its magnificence, his polemical writings are not more outside literature than Bear Mountain is outside New York State. His relation is no more astounding than Dubuffet's to painting.

What can we expect of Personism? (This is getting good, isn't it?) Everything, but we won't get it. It is too new, too vital a movement to promise anything. But it, like Africa, is on the way. The recent propagandists for technique on the one hand, and for content on the other, had better watch out.

[September 3, 1959; first published in *Yūgen* 7, 1961]

STATEMENT FOR *THE NEW AMERICAN POETRY*

I am mainly preoccupied with the world as I experience it, and at times when I would rather be dead the thought that I could never write another poem has so far stopped me. I think this is an ignoble attitude. I would rather die for love, but I haven't.

I don't think of fame or posterity (as Keats so grandly and genuinely did), nor do I care about clarifying experiences for anyone or bettering (other than accidentally) anyone's state or social relation, nor am I for any particular technical development in the American language simply because I find it necessary. What is happening to me, allowing for lies and exaggerations which I try to avoid, goes into my poems. I don't think my experiences are clarified or made beautiful for myself or anyone else, they are just there in whatever form I can find them. What is clear to me in my work is probably obscure to others, and vice versa. My formal "stance" is found at the crossroads where what I know and can't get meets what is left of that I know and can bear without hatred. I dislike a great deal of contemporary poetry — all of the past you read is usually quite great — but it is a useful thorn to have in one's side.

It may be that poetry makes life's nebulous events tangible to me and restores their detail; or conversely, that poetry brings forth the intangible quality of incidents which are all too concrete and circumstantial. Or each on specific occasions, or both all the time.

[1959]

STATEMENT FOR PATERSON SOCIETY

It is very difficult for me to write a statement for Paterson, much as I
would find it agreeable to do so if I could. So perhaps it could take the
form of a letter? and not be a real statement. Because if I did write a
statement it would probably be so non-pertinent to anything you might
want to know in connection with my actual poems. The only two starts
I have been able to think of since you first asked me for one, are (1) to
begin with a description of what I would like my poetry to be, or hope
it is (already? in the future? I don't know). This would be a description
of the effect other things have had upon me which I in my more day-
dreamy moments wish that I could effect in others. Well you can't have
a statement saying "My poetry is the Sistine Chapel of verse," or "My
poetry is just like Pollock, de Kooning and Guston rolled into one great
verb," or "My poetry is like a windy day on a hill overlooking the stormy
ocean" — first of all it isn't so far as I can tell, and secondly even if it
were something like all of these that wouldn't be because I managed to
make it that way. I couldn't, it must have been an accident, and I would
probably not recognize it myself. Further, what would poetry like that
be? It would have to be the Sistine Chapel itself, the paintings themselves,
the day and time specifically. Impossible.

Or (2) if I then abandoned that idea and wrote you about my convic-
tions concerning form, measure, sound, yardage, placement and ear —
well, if I went into that thoroughly enough nobody would ever want to
read the poems I've already written, they would have been so thoroughly
described, and I would have to do everything the opposite in the future
to avoid my own boredom, and where would I be? That's where I am
anyway, I suppose, but at least this way it's not self-induced. Besides, I
can't think of any more than one poem at a time, so I would end up with
a "poetics" based on one of my poems which any other poem of mine
would completely contradict except for certain affections or habits of
speech they might include. So that would be of no use for general readers,
and misleading for anyone who had already read any of my poems. So, as
they say in the Café Flore, it's better to *tas gueule.* I'm not giving up respon-
sibility for the poems. I definitely don't believe that "your idea is as good
as anyone's about what it means." But I don't want to make up a lot of
prose about something that is perfectly clear in the poems. If you cover
someone with earth and grass grows, you don't know what they looked

like any more. Critical prose makes too much grass grow, and I don't want to help hide my own poems, much less kill them.

I know you will think of the remarks I made for Don Allen's anthology and that "Manifesto" in LeRoi Jone's *Yūgen*. In the case of the manifesto I think it was all right because it was a little diary of my thoughts, after lunch with LeRoi walking back to work, about the poem I turned out to be just about to write ("Personal Poem," which he published in an earlier issue of *Yūgen*.) It was, as a matter of fact intended for Don Allen's anthology, and I was encouraged to write it because LeRoi told me at lunch that he had written a statement for the anthology. But Don Allen thought it unwise to use it in relation to the earlier poems included, quite rightly, so I wrote another which he did use. This latter, it seems to me now, is even more mistaken, pompous, and quite untrue, as compared to the manifesto. But it is also, like the manifesto, a diary of a particular day and the depressed mood of that day (it's a pretty depressing day, you must admit, when you feel you relate more importantly to poetry than to life), and as such may perhaps have more general application to my poetry since I have been more often depressed than happy, as far as I can tally it up. In the case of either, it's a hopeless conundrum: it used to be that I could only write when I was miserable; now I can only write when I'm happy. Where will it all end? At any rate, this will explain why I can't really say anything definite for the Paterson Society for the time being.

[March 16, 1961]

NEW DIRECTIONS IN MUSIC: MORTON FELDMAN*

The last ten years have seen American composers, painters and poets assuming leading roles in the world of international art to a degree hitherto unexpected. Led by the painters, our whole cultural milieu has changed and is still changing. The "climate" for receptivity to the new in art has improved correspondingly, and one of the most important aspects of this change has been the inter-involvement of the individual arts with one another. Public interest in the emergence of a major composer, painter or poet has, in recent years, almost invariably been preceded by his recognition among other painters, poets and musicians. The influence of esthetic ideas has also been mutual: the very extremity of the differences between the arts has thrown their technical analogies into sharp relief. As an example of what I mean by this, we find that making the analogy between certain all-over paintings of Jackson Pollock and the serial technique of Webern clarifies the one by means of the other — a seemingly "automatic" painting is seen to be as astutely controlled by the sensibility of Pollock in its assemblage of detail toward a unified experience as are certain of Webern's serial pieces. And it is interesting to note that initial public response to works by both artists was involved in bewilderment at the seeming "fragmentation" of experience. Although these analogies cease to be helpful if carried too far, it is in the framework of these mutual influences in the arts that Morton Feldman could cite, along with the playing of Fournier, Rachmaninoff and Tudor and the friendship of John Cage, the paintings of Philip Guston as important influences on his work. He adds, "Guston made me aware of the 'metaphysical place' which we all have but which so many of us are not sensitive to by previous conviction."

I interpret this "metaphysical place," this land where Feldman's pieces live, as the area where spiritual growth in the work can occur, where the form of a work may develop its inherent originality and the personal

* *Extensions I for Violin and Piano* (1951), *Structures for String Quartet* (1951), *Projection 4 for Violin and Piano* (1951) (graph), *Extensions 4 for Three Pianos* (1952-1953), *Intersection 3 for Piano* (1953) (graph), *Two Pieces for Two Pianos* (1954), *Three Pieces for String Quartet* (1954-1956), *Piece for Four Pianos* (1957); David Tudor, Russell Sherman, Edwin Hymovitz, pianists; Matthew Raimondi and Joseph Rabushka, violinists; Walter Trampler, violist; Seymour Barab, cellist, Columbia Records, 1959.

meaning of the composer may become explicit. In a more literal way it is the
space which must be cleared if the sensibility is to be free to express its in-
dividual preference for sound and to explore the meaning of this preference.
That the process of finding this metaphysical place of unpredictability and
possibliity can be a drastic one is witnessed by the necessity Feldman felt a
few years ago to avoid the academic ramifications of serial technique. Like
the artists involved in the new American painting, he was pursuing a per-
sonal search for expression which could not be limited by any system.

This is in sharp contrast to the development of many of Feldman's
European contemporaries, for example Boulez and Stockhausen, whose
process has tended toward elaboration and systematization of method.
Unlike Feldman's their works are eminently suited to analysis and what they
have lacked in sensuousness they invariably may regain in intellectual pro-
fundity and in the metaphysical implications of their methods. But if we
speak of a metaphysical place in relation to Feldman, it is the condition
under which the work was created and which is left behind the moment
a given work has been completed.

Feldman's decision to avoid the serial technique was an instinctive
attempt to avoid the clichés of the International School of present-day
avant-garde. He was not to become an American composer in the historical-
reminiscence line, but to find himself free of the conceptualized and self-
conscious modernity of the international movement. Paradoxically, it is
precisely this freedom which places Feldman in the front rank of the ad-
vanced musical art of our time.

A key work in the development away from serial technique is the *Inter-
section 3 for Piano* (1953). A graph piece, it is totally abstract in its every
dimension. Feldman here successfully avoids the symbolic aspect of sound
which has so plagued the abstract works of his contemporaries by employing
unpredictability reinforced by spontaneity — the score indicates "indeterm-
inacy of pitch" as a direction for the performer. Where others have attempted
to reverse or nullify this aural symbolism (loud-passion, soft-tenderness, and
so on) to free themselves, Feldman has created a work which exists without
references outside itself, "as if you're not listening, but looking at something
in nature." This is something serialism could not accomplish. This freedom is
shared by the performer to the extent that what he plays is not dictated be-
yond the graph "control" — the range of a given passage and its temporal
area and division are indicated, but the actual notes heard must come from
the performer's response to the musical situation. To perform Feldman's
graph pieces at all, the musician must reach the metaphysical place where

each can occur, allying necessity with unpredictability. Where a virtuoso work places technical demands upon the performer, a Feldman piece seeks to engage his improvisatory collaboration, with its call on musical creativity as well as interpretative understanding. The performance on this record is proof of how beautifully this can all work out; yet, the performer could doubtless find other beauties in *Intersection 3* on another occasion.

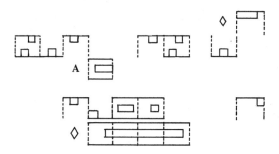

Projection 4 for Violin and Piano (1951) explores an entirely different area of musical experience. A graph piece also (see illustration), its marvellous austerity is achieved mainly through touch, and I will quote the note to the performer as an example of how the individual area of experience in these graph pieces is indicated to the performers:

NOTE:
the violin part is graphed above that for the piano. Dynamics are throughout equal and low.

For the violinist:
Timbre is indicated: ◇ = harmonic; P = pizzicato; A = arco. Relative pitch (high, middle, low) is indicated: ⊓ = high; ⊐⊏ = middle; ⊓ = low. Any tone within the ranges indicated may be sounded. The limits of these ranges may be freely chosen by the player. Multiple stops are indicated by numbers within the squares. Duration is indicated by the amount of space taken up by the square or rectangle, each box (:　:) being potentially 4 icti. The single ictus or pulse is at the tempo of 72 or thereabouts.

For the pianist:
The ◇ indicates playing without sounding (for the release of har-
monics). Pitches, their number and duration are indicated as for the
violinist.

A comparison of these two graph pieces, whose ambiances are so to-
tally dissimilar, gives an idea of the great compositional flexibility pos-
sible with graph notation.

Unpredictability is used in a different way still in the *Piece for Four
Pianos* (1957). This work, scored in notation rather than graph, begins
simultaneously for all four pianos, after which the following notes may
be played to the end by each of the pianists at time intervals of their
mutual or individual choice. Feldman has said, "The repeated notes are
not musical pointillism, as in Webern, but they are where the mind rests
on an image — the beginning of the piece is like a recognition, not a
motif, and by virtue of the repetitions it conditions one to listen." As
we proceed to experience the individual time-responses of the four
pianists we are moving inexorably toward the final image where the
mind can rest, which is the end of the piece. In this particular perform-
ance it is as if one were traversing an enormous plain at the opposite
ends of which were two huge monoliths, guarding its winds and grasses.

In all of Feldman's recent work the paramount image is that of touch
— "the use of the instrument must be as sensitive as the application of
paint on canvas." (Which brings us back to Rachmaninoff, Fournier and
Tudor.) In some pieces the entrance into the rhythmic structure is left
entirely to the performer, and it is in this area that unpredictability en-
ters and the performer must create the experience within the limits of
the notation.

On the other hand, one of the most remarkable pieces recorded here
is *Structures for String Quartet* (1951). It is a classical string quartet
without sonata development, without serial development, in general
without benefit of clergy. Like Emily Dickinson's best poems, it does
not seem to be what it is until all questions of "seeming" have disappeared
in its own projection. Its form reveals itself after its meaning is revealed,
as Dickinson's passion ignores her dazzling technique. As with several
other Feldman pieces, if you cannot hear *Structures*, I doubt that study-
ing the score would be a help, though it is a thoroughly notated field of
dynamic incident, whose vertical elements are linked by a sort of shy
contrapuntal stimulation of great delicacy and tautness.

In an *oeuvre* which so insistently provides unpredictability with opportunities for expansion and breath, the question of notation at all arises, for the graph would seem to provide an adequate control for the experience and a maximum of differentiation. But differentiation is not Feldman's point, even in the graph music: the structure of the piece is never the image, nor in eschewing precise notation of touch is Feldman leaving the field open for dramatic incident whereby the structure could become an image (as in Boulez). Notation is, then, not so much a rigid exclusion of chance, but the means of preventing the structure from becoming an image in these works, and an indication of the composer's personal preference for where unpredictability should operate. As John Cage remarked in this connection, "Feldman's conventionally notated music is himself playing his graph music." And of course the degree of precision in the notation is directly related to the nature of the musical experience Feldman is exposing. This notation can be very precise, as in *Extensions 1 for Violin and Piano* (1951), which indicates an increasing tempo of inexorable development from beginning to end by metronomic markings, as well as the dynamics and expressive development.

Although the traditionally notated works are in the majority on this record (*Extensions 1*, *Structures for String Quartet*, *Extensions 4*, *Two Pieces for Two Pianos*, *Three Pieces for String Quartet*), I have gone into the use of unpredictability in this music at such length in order to reach a distinction about its use in much contemporary music. In Feldman's work unpredictability involves the performer and the audience much in the same way it does the composer, inviting an increase of sensitivity and intensity. But in much of the extreme vanguard music in America and Europe, particularly that utilizing tape and electronic devices along with elements of unpredictability, the statistical unpredictability has occurred in the traditional manner during the making of the piece; it has been employed preconceptually as a logical outgrowth of serial technique, and it is dead by the time you hear it, though the music is alive in the traditional sense of hearing. What Feldman is assuming, and it is a courageous assumption, is that the performer is a sensitive and inspired musician who has the best interests of the work at heart. This attitude leaves him free to concentrate on the main inspiration-area where the individual piece is centered.

What he finds in these centers — whether it is the sensuousness of tone and the cantilena-like delicacy of breathing in *Three Pieces for String Quartet* (1954-56), or the finality of the "dialogues" in *Exten-*

sions 4 for Three Pianos (1952-53) — is on each occasion a personal and profound revelation of the inner quality of sound. The works recorded here already are an important contribution to the music of the 20th century. Whether notated or graphed, his music sets in motion a spiritual life which is rare in any period and especially so in ours.

DAVID SMITH: THE COLOR OF STEEL

The Terminal Iron Works in Bolton Landing, N. Y., has become by now a landmark in American art. You drive out of town into the hills and meadows and the T.I.W., as the signs for turnoffs say, is in a hollow beside the road at the entrance to the drive which dips down at the studio and then climbs up the hill to David Smith's house. When I was there recently the studio held one large unfinished sculpture (welded but unpainted) and three others in various stages of progression. Outside the studio huge piles of steel lay waiting to be used, and along the road up to the house a procession of new works, in various stages of painting, stood in the attitudes of some of Smith's characteristic titles: they stood there like a *Sentinel* or *Totem*, or *Ziggurat*, not at all menacing, but very aware.

The process of painting the sculptures is a complicated one: the very large ones, which is to say almost all the ones done recently, require more than twenty coats, including several of rust-resistant paint of the kind used on battleships, and many coats of undercolor to hide the brilliant orange-yellow of the basic coats; these undercoats frequently give a velvety texture to the surface (like the iron hand in the velvet glove), and eventually disappear under a final color or colors, or show through, as Smith conceives the final piece. In some cases parts of a piece will be painted different colors, only to disappear under an overall layer of paint as the ultimate image emerges.

The house commands a magnificent view of the mountains and its terrace overlooks a meadow "fitted" with cement bases on which finished stainless steel and painted sculptures were standing. Around the other sides of the house more unfinished works were placed for Smith to ponder. The effect of all these works along the road and around the house was somewhat that of people who are awaiting admittance to a formal reception and, while they wait, are thinking about their roles when they join the rest of the guests already in the meadow.

The contrast between the sculptures and this rural scene is striking: to see a cow or a pony in the same perspective as one of the *Ziggurats*, with the trees and mountains behind, is to find nature soft and art harsh; nature looks intimate and vulnerable, the sculptures powerful, indomitable. Smith's works in galleries have often looked rugged and in-the-American-grain, which indeed they are in some respects, but at Bolton Landing the sophistication of vision and means comes to the fore strongly. Earlier works, mounted on pedestals or stones about the terrace and garden, seem to partake of the physical atmosphere, but the recent works assert an authoritative presence over the panorama of mountains, divorced from nature by the insistence of their individual personalities, by the originality of their scale and the exclusion of specific references to natural forms.

For twenty-five years Smith has been at the forefront of the sculptural avant-garde, in quality if not that long in reputation. Like Arshile Gorky, Smith took, assimilated, synthesized and made personal many developments in international modern art movements which had hitherto not found their way into American sculpture without a nullifying gaucherie. Because of the far-reaching effects of these explorations, Smith has sometimes been mistaken for an eclectic artist, but this is not at all the case. His has not been a taming of the impulses discovered in the germinal works of the first half of the century, but a roughening, a broadening, a sharpening of usage, depending on his needs at the time. And in so doing, Smith brought out aspects of the sculpture of Picasso, Gonzalez and Giacometti which had before seemed minor, if not entirely hidden.

But this was in the early work. The new sculptures are of painted steel, of stainless steel or of bronze. The bronzes are least different from earlier work of Smith, though they face that medium with new images in mind. The stainless steel sculptures continue a direction which first reached monumental proportions in *Fifteen Planes* (shown at the Venice Biennale, 1958). They are tall, glittering, leggy works, usually with several flat surfaces meeting like still-lifes above the verticals which hold them aloft. Seen in full sunlight, with the stainless steel *Sentinels* which continue another direction of his work, their polished and ground surfaces carry the eye over highly elaborate changes of tone without violating the flatness of the plane. They look severe and dashing; to continue the meadow-party idea, they are the sort of people who are about to walk away because you just aren't as interesting as they are, but they're not quite mean enough to do it. The working of the surface in this medium, as Smith does it, has the kind of severe, ironic frivolity Velasquez brought to the marvelously detailed costume of a mean-looking Spanish nobleman. But of course it is really all a matter of light, light sinking, light dashing into the surface, light bouncing back at you.

Many of the painted works are also monumental in size. Unlike Calder or Nakian, or for that matter his own previous painted sculpture, Smith does not usually use a single color for a whole piece here, unless it is opaque enough to let variations and undertones show through. Nor is the color usually applied to separate parts, but rather to shift their functions as visual elements of a single image. In some pieces the color spreads over one plane onto a segment of the next and then to a third, like a drape partially concealing a nude. This is no longer the constructivist intersection of colored planes, nor is the color used as a means of unifying the surface. Unification is approached by inviting the eye to travel over the complicated surface exhaustively, rather than inviting it to settle on the whole first and then explore details. It is the esthetic of culmination rather than examination. Smith uses modeling in some areas; over-painting where the whole surface of a form vibrates with the undercolor; effects of the brush; the interchange of color areas with the parts of the steel construction of which they expound the quality and ring changes on the structure. Sometimes the reference is directly to a specific painting, as in the piece dedicated to Kenneth Noland, which presents its three-dimensional head like a target whose rings had been pushed and pulled out of kilter, as if in answer to the painter's request for a three-dimensional version of himself. But it is never sculpture *being* painting, it is sculpture looking at painting and responding in its own fashion. In a world where everything from sponges dipped in paint to convertibles crushed into shapes by power presses have been put to sculptural usage, this new development in Smith's work is, oddly enough, the boldest and most original statement about the nature of sculptural perception. On the simplest level he has focused new attention on the plastic forces within the metal by providing a determinable surface (paint) which does not violate its nature, or by working the stainless steel surfaces with the freedom that belongs to drawing paper; on the more complicated visual level of communicatory imagery he has extended the expressive possibilities of three-dimensional forms.

Using the inspiration of the material's quality as a start, Smith does not hesitate to urge change, advancement or concealment, as the image of a particular work takes form. Having contemplated the materials at length, he bears no relation to the sensitive person staring soulfully at a seashell, driftwood or a nail, and taking it home never to *see* it again, a trap which not every "assemblage" sculptor manages to avoid. He is brutal enough to be bored and ashamed enough to be ambitious. He has no false humility before the material world, and asks no humility of it. In the works which used "found" objects, such as the *Agricola* series, the impulse was not to cherish the "poetry" of the part, but to give it a presence according to what its formal function might become. He never makes memorabilia. Nor does he ask the materials to be attractive, just to co-operate.

The logic of Smith's move from painting (1927) to three-dimensional objects and then to sculpture in the following six years has been well examined elsewhere. From the first he occasionally used paint on his sculp-

tures. But there is no evidence from the way the sculptures were painted
that the painting of them represented any nostalgia for the act of painting it-
self. The interest, from the beginning works of 1933 on, seems to have been
in the control of the look of the surface as it performed to create the whole:
a typical example of what I mean is the *Egyptian Landscape* of 1951, where
the red paint on the steel parts creates the feeling of the somber heat of mol-
ten metal, and the Nile-green of the painted bronze forms summons a more
hieratic quality than bronze patinas usually provide. But thinking over some
of the works of other periods in his development, most of the painted pieces
seem as much patinaed as painted: they do not stand apart by virtue of the
different means employed. A work incorporating found parts, like *The Five
Spring*, with a rusty patina (none of them are actually rusted), presents a
greater difference in color quality when compared to blue-patinaed bronzes
like *O Drawing*, than when compared to *Pillar of Sunday* or *Australia*, though
the latter are painted, respectively, red and black. Again, in the *Iron Woman*
of 1954-58, the faint rubbings of yellow in the scratches and abrasions of the
oval planes point up the silkiness of the stainless steel as a quality of the metal
itself, not as the introduction of an enhancing element which is foreign to it.
But the fact that the painted pieces were painted does already have a signifi-
cance which bears on the more recent work: apparently Smith intends to pre-
serve the look of these pieces as close to their first moment of completion as
possible, to preserve the state of the sculpture's original inception. If one of
them should rust or be nicked, he would strip it down to the bare metal and
restore it to its original color and texture. It is interesting that he is not tempt-
ed to alter a given piece in the light of subsequent developments of his own
sensibility, he simply makes sure that its own being is intact.

Smith has always been known for his esthetic curiosity and inventiveness,
for rapid and drastic changes in style whenever the new interest seized him.
The new painted steel works are not so much the result of a change in out-
look as outgrowths of several non-conflicting ideas in the recent past, particu-
larly the *Tank Totems* and the *Sentinels.* They move into a scale which he
had never previously been able to afford and for which he is fully equipped.
They have an odd atmosphere of grandeur and, at the same time, delight,
like seeing a freshly washed elephant through the eyes of a child: the *Zig-
gurats* in particular induce a sort of naive wonder which lasts long after one
has left them. Despite the size of these works, they have an atmosphere of
affection for the huge slabs of steel, for the hoisting and welding of them,
for the impulse to see them join and rise. Smith once said if he had the
money he'd like to make a sculpture as big as a locomotive, and I think if

Smith were asked to make a real locomotive he wouldn't care if it ever ran so long as he had the use of all that metal. The humor which had previously characterized Smith's work at certain times, often sarcastic or satiric, now seems to have been transformed into this delight towards the material and, coupled with the formidable structural achievement of the works, gives them an amiability and a dignity which is the opposite of pretentiousness. In addition to the formal uses to which paint is put, mentioned above, I consider that the painting of these pieces also represents a sort of diary of the development of the forms: in each piece he has gathered together the separate impulses of the construction of the parts by the notation of the painted surfaces, so that as the formal functioning of a plane changes as the total image demands it to function in a different way, the painting of it will have some of the quality of the original inspiration for its existence. There is then the interplay of the steel forms, as they relate strictly to the elements of the construction, with the memory of these forms, provided by the paint, resonantly adding to the formal structure the feelings of the artist as he worked.

Smith had already made a considerable success in this direction with his early *Helmholtzian Landscape*, but these new works move into an area of seemingly infinite exploration. Smith wants to do a great deal in each sculpture, as an artist he is very inclusive, and this development provides him with the range and the means to give us everything he wants. The best of the current sculptures didn't make me feel I wanted to *have* one, they made me feel I wanted to *be* one.

[*Art News*, December 1961]

ART CHRONICLE I

The other day I was at the Guggenheim Museum to see the ABSTRACT
EXPRESSIONISTS AND IMAGISTS show again, but before going into
the show itself it may be worthwhile, or at least different, to say some-
thing nice about the building itself. From long before construction work
started on it, it had been a controversial thing, and it stayed so through-
out the work on it, its opening, and its first several shows — every detail
of its design was discussed everywhere from the newspaper to The Club,
and rumors that its then-director might quit because he hated the floor,
or the wall, or the dome, or the lighting, or even the elevator, were circu-
lated. (He did leave subsequently, but apparently not because of F.L.W.)
The Museum is, of course, worthy of all this attention, and it has many
merits not shared by other institutions of a similar or identical nature
(and a few disadvantages: I don't like bumping into those pillars when
I'm talking to somebody): it's wonderful looking from the outside, and
when you enter the flat exhibition space on the ground floor the effect
of the works near at hand, the ramps and over them glimpses of canvases,
and then the dome, is urbane and charming, like the home of a cultivated
and mildly eccentric person. The elevator is a good idea too; I wonder if
anyone has ever taken it down? And apart from the one-way thing about
it, it takes off the curse of most elevators, which is that when you go up
in an elevator in the day-time you are usually going to some unpleasant
experience like work or a job interview, but here you are going up for
pleasure. When you get to the top, and before beginning the descent (an
opposite experience from that of Dante, since most often the important
works are hung down in the "straight" gallery just above the main level),
you used to get a miniature retrospective of Kandinsky from the Museum's
own collection, and right now there is a rather mute and interesting small
show of newspapers, letters (as in H and F), and books by Chryssa. The
downward stroll, then, is enhanced by the glimpses you've been sneaking
(from the top this time) at the pictures on the lower ramps, and you get
lots of surprises: things that looked especially inviting or dramatic from
a partial look turn out to be totally uninteresting and others you hadn't
bothered to anticipate are terrific (though this operation isn't invariable).
Finally about this ramp, it almost completely eliminates the famous
gallery-going fatigue. Your back doesn't ache, your feet don't hurt, and
the light on the paintings, the variety of distance chosen for them to be

against or away from the wall and towards you, is usually quite judicious
– people who find it so hard to "see" the picture in the lighting of the
Guggenheim should try going to the average studio in which most New
York artists work before they complain. (I know museums aren't supposed
to be studios, I'm talking about looking at really good paintings or sculp-
tures, which frequently has little to do with locale or condition.) Anyhow,
I like the whole experience, the "bins" where you come around a semi-
wall and find a masterpiece has had its back to you, the relation between
seeing a painting or a sequence of them from across the ramp and then
having a decent interval of time and distraction intervene before the close
scrutiny: in general my idea is that this may not be (as what is) the ideal
museum, but in this instance Frank Lloyd Wright was right in the lovable
way that Sophie Tucker was to get her gold tea set, which she described
as, "It's way out on the nut for service, but it was my dream!"

New York gallery-goers are used to feeling that no matter what they
are looking at, the institution in question will dish it up to them with the
appropriate importance so far as installation goes, hence the accusation
that the Guggenheim makes certain paintings look inferior to their in-
trinsic quality. This is of course a fallacy: position in installation and
lighting has nothing to do with esthetic importance. Actually, the only
truly important new works to be shown in New York last and this
season were the Matisse cut-outs at the Museum of Modern Art, and they
could have been hung outdoors in the garden without jeopardizing their im-
portance in the slightest (so long as it didn't rain). I am not saying that
the abstract show at the Guggenheim shouldn't have been hung differently,
since certain pictures did kill their neighbors and vice versa, but it had no-
thing to do with positioning for strategic importance. But the Bonnard in
the Guggenheim's first show after its opening did not suffer from the light
and the position, as often remarked, it is simply a property of Bonnard's
mature work, and one of its most fragile charms, to look slightly washed-
out, to look what every sophisticated person let alone artist wants to look:
a little "down," a little effortless and helpless. He was never a powerful
painter, per se.

At the opening of the abstract show at the Guggenheim several people
were going around saying, "At last it looks like a real museum here,"
which is a terribly funny notion when you think that the abstract expres-
sionist movement is basically anti-museum in spirit, and its members were
the only organized group to send out a letter of protest about the museum
to the newspapers even before construction on the building had begun. The

thing is that with this show the Guggenheim became part of New York, in that it featured New York's favorite art movement. And no matter how much Wright himself may have hated painting and sculpture, the physical setup of the building does nothing to hurt that movement.

The selection is another matter: what the title implies is a summary of achievement, but what you get is recent works by most of the important members of the movement. This is very interesting, if you want to look at paintings. Unfortunately many people wanted to see a justification, packaged in a new Sherry's container, with a card saying, "Because of this show you are entitled to keep on admiring abstract expressionism." Hence the criticism the Guggenheim has gotten about the quality of the show, some of it near hysteria: "A WEAK HOFMANN! HOW COULD THEY!" None of the reviewers seems to have thought, "How could he!"

What does happen in the show, without disturbing anybody's reputation, is a shift in the emphasis of who is doing the interesting work: some artists maintain their vitality, others look terribly dull, younger members zoom to the fore, all on the fore-admitted basis of one recent work, so no images are toppled permanently. This is a perfectly fair thing to have happen and gives the show an air of free-wheeling accuracy. This is all living art and the show reflects the living situation: just as Al Held and Joan Mitchell and Philip Guston will absorb the imagination of one season, so do Michael Goldberg and Robert Motherwell and Franz Kline another. It depends on what you see and when it's shown and it keeps you fresh for looking and for the excitement of art. A lot of people would like to see art dead and sure, but you don't see them up at the Cloisters reading Latin.

The present show also, precisely because it is mainly made up of recent works, reflects another very human situation; the relation between artists of a given tendency is frequently very close. Why this should be a matter of concern to anyone but the artists themselves is beyond me, since the alternatives to this fortuitous happening are blindness or hypocrisy. Nevertheless, the viewer should make more distinctions than the artist, he has time and room for it, he is merely looking and experiencing, where the artist is creating something, whether in his own or another's image, no small feat in either case.

In a capitalist country fun is everything. Fun is the only justification for the acquisitive impulse, if one is to be honest. (The Romans were honest, they thought it was all girls, grapes and snow.) The Guggenheim Museum is fun, and as such it justifies itself. Abstract expressionism is not, and its justifications must be found elsewhere. Not to say it as justification, but simply as fact, abstract expressionism is the art of serious men. They are serious because they are *not* isolated. So out of this populated cavern of self come brilliant, uncomfortable works, works that don't reflect you or your life, though you can know them. Art is not *your* life, it is someone else's. Something very difficult for the acquisitive spirit to understand, and for that matter the spirit of joinership that animates communism. But it's there.

So what's good in this show and how does it look? Well it *looks* very good, as a matter of fact it looks better than it is. Not wanting to do a hugger-mugger in the Louvre, the dross always is self-effacing and disappears. So you are left with some terrific stuff:

one of the most interesting Brooks' in years, where the artist's exceptional skill at handling paint masses is roughened up somewhat and gets to a kind of baroque literalness, joining Clyfford Still in his firmness about stopping-points;

a magnificent Motherwell, the kind of painting that everyone must dream of doing if they want to do anything at all: it has everything, it shimmers with a half-concealed light, it draws when it wants to, and withal it has an opulence and a majesty which is completely uncharacteristic of the American sensibility unless you think your mother went to bed with an Indian;

earlier I hinted at Al Held's show at the Poindexter Gallery last season, and his picture is terrifc here — he is a wonderful artist, at the same time sensitive and blunt, related, and how gratifyingly, to the Gorky of the late 30s, and he is a clearer of the eye and mind; Held reminds you that color, form, shape (and there is a difference between form and shape), and nuance are still not giving the game over to the enemy — you don't have to become a clock anymore if you're near a Held, he is not painting about position in time;

the Raymond Parker looked very beautiful and I for one hope that I never see another Parker with a thick gold band around it. It crowds the space too much, it falsifies the delicate balance and subtle correspondence of his near tones, and it is to the credit of the Guggenheim that it took it the way it was, though why the same manner wasn't adopted for his one-man show there earlier this year I can't imagine, even if it did manage to be impressive despite this handicap;

in relation to the other examples, I think the wrong Frankenthaler was chosen, expert as it is, for the content of the show, but more about her

later. The Rauschenberg ditto, because if you think he should be in the
show at all, it is as an imagist rather than an expressionist (both should
be preceded by an abstract-, natch), and he should have been represented
in force rather than in retirement, as is true in another way of the hangings
of the Joan Mitchell and the Alfred Leslie, who are too sure of hand and
distinguished of spirit to suffer this treatment without a sullen smile —
one must simply see them elsewhere, yet they make their presence felt
or I wouldn't mention them;

de Kooning has shown several single pictures recently of such a beauty
that one wonders, if he ever does get around to having a show of the new
abstractions, whether the Sidney Janis Gallery won't just go into an apoth-
eosis, and the one here is no exception — I wish I could give credence to
the next remark by thinking of a single indifferent work by de Kooning
but I can't so here goes anyway: he is the greatest painter after Picasso
and Miró;

but not to run on, the *hits* of the show are mostly on the "mezzanine"
floor, the flat gallery where the absolutely superb Pollock, Still and New-
man establish an aristocracy for American art which is unequalled any-
where, in the developments after World War II.

Where else is the big, brave art happening? Certainly not in Paris, where
artisanship has claimed and cured even the most demented intentions to
the point where seeing Helen Frankenthaler's recent show, or a single
fugitive Kline, or something from the Spanish School (Tapiés or Canogar
or Saura), is a sock in the eye along the rue de Seine. Of the younger gen-
eration there is only Riopelle, a gigantic spirit, with Soulages and Alechin-
sky trailing formalistically (and authentically) up towards the stars.

A lot of interesting things are happening right here which make Paris
and Rome seem quite dull and insensitive by comparison. There is, of
course, the construction-of-esthetic-objects movement, which since the
exhibition at the Museum of Modern Art will probably be designated
fairly clearly as assemblagists. This is a very courageous direction be-
cause it deliberately vies with the fondness one feels for a found object,
challenging in intimacy as well as structure all the autobiographical
associations that a found object embodies. In Claes Oldenburg's recent
exhibition THE STORE (107 East 2nd Street — the best thing since
L. L. BEAN), you find cakes your mother never baked, letters you
never received, jackets you never stole when you broke into that apart-
ment, and a bride that did not pose for Rembrandt's famous Jewish

ceremony. Somehow Oldenburg is the opposite of Britain's "kitchen sink" school: he can make a stove (with roast) or a lunch-counter display case lyrical, not to say magical. And he actually does do what is most often claimed wrongly in catalog blurbs: transform his materials into something magical and strange. If Red Grooms was the poet of this tendency and Jim Dine is the realist, then Oldenburg is the magician. His enormous cardboard figure at the Green Gallery, with its great legs stretched toward one on the floor, was sheer necromancy. Compared to these three artists, and adding to it Lucas Samaras and George Brecht, the European artists exploring this field are very dull. And the direction in itself must be taken quite apart from the work of Jasper Johns or Jean Follette or Robert Rauschenberg, each of whom has a separate and individual tradition behind their work, no matter what their influence may have joined together.

Rauschenberg had recently a very beautiful show at the Castelli Gallery and one unprecedented to my knowledge. It began as a group show, and gradually more Rauschenbergs moved in, while other works moved amiably out, as if to say, "Okay, Bob, this turn seems right for you, so take it, maestro, from Bar R." It was a beautiful show, and an event more interesting than many of the "happenings" down town. The gallery kept changing the paintings, which gave an unusual urgency to gallery-going. If I hadn't been very lucky, I would have missed seeing *Blue Eagle,* a modern work which nobody should be deprived of. One should add that his (our) experience of the *Dante Illustrations* which Rauschenberg exhibited last year have left none of us less the richer for any occasion in the future. Doré had never the pertinence for his society that those works have for ours, nor the beauty, nor the perception. So we all have that, too.

In the opposite camp, the "tradition of the new" traditional abstract-expressionist movement, lie Norman Bluhm's paintings, although jet or explode may be a more accurate word. A great deal has been written about the influence of Pollock, but that is all about the *look*, the technique which is best known (Pollock had several). Bluhm is the only artist working in the idiom of abstract-expressionism who has a spirit similar to that of Pollock, which is to say that he is *out* — beyond beauty, beyond compositon, beyond the old-fashioned kind of pictorial ambition. And Jasper Johns is somehow in this area, a very misunderstood artist, whose art presents to many something easily assimilable and understood, but Johns is one of the most mysterious artists of our time, an artist whose

work is *not* formal, in the sense that it is understood and expounded. He
has the experience, which may or may not be unfortunate for him, of seeing
his paintings greeted with delight because the images are recognizable when
they are filled with pain. At least that is one way of feeling them: one may
say that the meticulously and sensually painted rituals of imagery express
a profound boredom, in the Baudelairean sense, with the symbols of an
oversymbolic society, as Oedipus unconsciously exposed the errors of a
familial sentimentality based on disgust.

Bluhm's art, on the other hand, and they are arbitrarily juxtaposed, has
the other Grecian impulse which inspired fountains, temples and conquest.
Johns's business is to resist desire, Bluhm unconsciously inspires it. But
more, of course, must be thought about both.

[*Kulchur* II:5, Spring 1962]

ART CHRONICLE II

Certainly one of the wisest and most successful commissions given in
many years by a public institution was that to Reuben Nakian for the
façade sculpture recently installed on the outside of the Loeb Study Cen-
ter. New York University is to be congratulated on its sagacity and on its
daring in choosing this magnificent but totally unofficial sculptor. Like
huge metal leaves, the forms drift across the brick surface of the front of
the building facing Washington Square from the south, changing fantastic-
ally with the changing light of the day. Full sunlight and dawn viewings
are particularly to be recommended, if that doesn't sound too Lady
Murasaki.

Nakian has come to the fore in recent years with exciting momentum.
His career has been somewhat parallel to that of William Carlos Williams:
decades of ardent appreciation by "the happy few" and then BOOM! The
signal for this development was Charles Egan's presentation of a huge
black metal sculpture at the Stewart-Marean Gallery and then at his own
re-established gallery, on East 79th Street: this work, *The Rape of Lucrece,*
is a major achievement of 20th century sculpture. The two abstract fig-
ures are delineated by great scooping sheets of black, the one reclining
half-amorously, half-terrified, the other pressing rigidly, haltingly, with
the static, fixed posture of habitual lust. Around, through and about these
figures thrust the black rods which in a less original conception would be
armature, but here are formal elements of the sculpture, contrasting sharp-
ly with the concave and convex planes of the sheets forcing the eye to
shoot around or into the volumes, halting the imagination from straying
from esthetics into eroticism. This is a monumental work (the greatest di-
mension is 13 feet) in feeling as well as size. It was removed on extended
loan to the stairwell of the Museum of Modern Art and placed on view
for several months, after which it travelled to São Paulo, Brazil, as part of
Nakian's section in the U.S. representation at the VI Bienal. If one of the
world fairs doesn't show it, it's a crime.

Nor has Nakian one arrow to his bow: in the welded sculptures, the
cast bronzes, the terracottas, he is an undeniable master, imaginatively as
technically. The new works in plaster now at the Egan Gallery, which will
be cast in bronze later, are three major pieces too; to the grace and dignity
of the earlier black steel *Duchess of Alba* has been added a tone of calam-
itous tragedy in the two new *Trojan Women*; the proud amorousness of

the earlier black steel *Mars and Venus* has opened in the new *Olympia* to a grand, frivolous sexuality, cheerfully baroque in feeling.

Downstairs at the Egan Gallery is yet another Nakian exhibition devoted to his ideas for a fountain project. A large plaster *Voyage to Crete* is featured, which needs only casting to make it one of the most beautiful fountains in the New World. It is, as is much of his work, based on the Abduction of Europa by the Bull motif, and while it is abstract leaves no doubt where the water comes in. Surrounding and accompanying it, are a bevy of small terracottas, using the natural color with white and blue paint, more figurative than the large project, and summoning up visions of a modern Fragonard *cum* Bernini. Each of these small terracottas is absolutely enchanting, they move, they breathe, they cavort and swim or swoon: Nakian has discovered a delight in sculpture which is direct, immediate and lasting. He has none of the dogmatism of less sure innovators, nor is he a hedonist in the handling of his media. The accumulation of Nakian's reputation has been a slow, but unerring, process. He has been as much a part, as a sculptor, of the atmosphere of the great abstract-expressionists as has David Smith: at the Egan Gallery in the late 40s and early 50s his *Aphrodite,* and later *La Chambre à coucher de l'empereur,* were on more or less permanent view, sinking into the consciousnesses which were first receiving the message from de Kooning, Kline, Guston, Tworkov, Vincente, and so on, striking his discordant, provocative note to refresh the eye for the visions of others. Now that eye belongs to him at last and he is filling it with marvels. We already know some of the plans for Lincoln Center and I don't intend to go into them. But surely if the City Fathers, increasingly more ominous than Big Brother, must deprive us of so much, they could at least consider creating one major out-door sculptural situation which would provide pleasure, beauty, lubricity, and an insight which is not governed by previously approved geometrical panaceas. If my anxiety drives me to the need for an assuring hand, I want that hand to belong to a Pollock, a de Kooning, a David Smith, a Nakian, not to some astute logician. If you give a "square" to the public in the form of an unavoidable public adornment, it will take a lot of Shakespeare and Pirandello to keep from getting a thousand-fold squares back. So what's the center for anyway? is it an Arlington Cemetery dedicated to Man-and-God-at-Yale?

All right, *pace.* But it is imperative for Lincoln Center to have *some* outdoor sculptures, because the announced price of tickets is apparently going to prohibit us from seeing *any* of the indoor commissions. As a matter of fact, it is impossible to drop the subject there: the question of what and who at the Center, where sculpture is concerned, should be a nagging worry for everyone. Modern American sculpture is presently at a very great height of development: what other country today can offer us such a splendid and brilliant array of masters and those just on the brink of that accolade? Most of these men, as in the case of Smith and Nakian, either have executed, or have projected, work of a scale and grandeur which cannot at present be accommodated in either our public or private situations for one reason or another — and one prime reason is public and private ignorance of their value. Lincoln Center is one of the few foreseeable possibilities to rectify this situation and, in so doing, allow our sculptors to make real their dreams, dreams which follow so closely Keats' great aspiration: "I am ambitious of doing the world some good." All right, to prove what marvelous possibilities could be in store for us I should "name names," so, allowing for possible omissions which the Center authorities can easily fill in, let us imagine Lincoln Center with major sculptural works by at least the following artists: Smith, Nakian, Ferber, Agostini, Roszak, Lipton, Spaventa, Mark di Suvero, Chamberlain, Stankiewicz . . . Take it from there! (And why not purchase or borrow the Lipchitz *Joie de Vivre?*) With a combination of intelligence and daring, how could Lincoln Center fail to become the sculptural center of the United States?

Well, *that* situation holds at least the possiblity of saving, but some really sad news is the announcement of its last season by the Tanager Gallery. This artists' co-operative gallery has been the most distinguished in the 10th Street area for several years, one where each year at Christmas time its invitational exhibition showed small works by the most illustrious names in contemporary American painting alongside lesser or totally unknown ones to the benefit of all; these were big shows hung with extraordinary taste and discernment. At other times of the year the Tanager has given one-man shows to a roster of artists any uptown gallery would be proud to boast, and indeed many of the artists have moved up there. At random one finds that such artists as Alex Katz, Lois Dodd, Sally Hazelet, Gabriel Kohn, Al Jensen, John Grillo, George Ortman, Philip Pearlstein, Angelo Ippolito, Charles Cajori, Sidney Geist . . . well, a list of artists who've shown there is available from the gallery for the curious, and it's a very impressive one. The member artists who have struggled through the vicissitudes of keeping a gallery open for ten years may not get their just reward, but they should get a lot of praise and gratitude. The Tanager, through the high quality of its exhibitions over the years, and through the fact that its exhibitions were chosen by a group of artists with little or no possibility of, let alone interest in, commercial values, was able to confer on a first show by an unknown artist a distinction pretty much unavailable to the younger artist elsewhere.

Getting back to sculpture, the Tanager recently showed a very interesting group of "flat sculptures" by Alex Katz. These figures are very original in scale, ranging from a life-size girl in a blue bathing-suit (who is nude behind) to a series of small cutout figures of the same man hanging on the wall, walking away from us, receding in the flat distance. They are beautifully and wittily painted, which is characteristic of Katz's paintings proper as well, and the larger, free-standing figures bear some resemblance to the Dummy-Board Figures which stood by English firesides of the late 17th and early 18th centuries to give burglars the illusion that the rooms were occupied. In contrast, Katz's figures are modern in ethos, emphasizing almost inadvertently the spatial absence which surrounds them; his concern for hard, no-nonesense paint quality and usually for strong "close" values in color give his figures a physically flat and psychologically adament stance which points up the fine accuracy of his paint handling.

Yet because of their strange reality a little of the 17th century aura remains in some of the male figures, provoking the poet Bill Berkson to remark, "He's a dumb-watchman — you know, like a dumb-waiter or a dumb-valet." They have an air of watchfulness, without ever being silhouettes.

On first acquaintance these "flat sculptures" are surprising, though the fact that Katz is the one to create them is not. He is a marvelous "flattener" of canvas, too, and one of the most individual sensibilities in the New York School — which is to say that his work is original and he lives in New York. Katz's "world" of painting has been expanding and, paradoxically, strengthening steadily since his 1959 show, and the two last shows at the Stable Gallery saw him in full force. He has a number of fortes: landscapes which have an iron hand inside their velvet glove; portraits which reveal the mysteriousness of personal appearance rather than a sympathetic response to character; figures isolated in a "field" of color which do not float or pose, but expound that simplest and often least realized of pictorial causalities, that the environment of the painted figure is the paint itself whether with or without atmosphere or delineation of locale. He seems attracted to verges (of prettiness, of amiability, of lushness, of corn), but always leaps beyond. Beneath the obviously attractive qualities of his work, characteristics of simplicity, sincerity and straightforward seeing, there is a great deal of stubbornness and even arrogance, which keeps them themselves and him his own man. He is probably the only one among us who could do a real *Joie de vivre* which would be neither sentimental nor forced, judging by his large red-haired nude in the forest, and again by his boat, all in brilliant green and blue, which looks as if it were waiting for the drunken Rimbaud to jump in and shove off. In yet another aspect of his work, Katz employs an apparently instinctive, and certainly subtle, geometrical principle which gives rightness and candor to the figure's relation with the surface and with its boundaries or limits, which he makes even clearer in the paintings where the figure is encircled by a second color which in turn terminates in the limits of the canvas. Katz is thus able to ring extraordinary color changes with the figure, the circular or oval area, and the "outer" color which ends at the rectangular canvas edges, since none of these areas ever becomes simply a framer, as they do in tintypes, for instance. Elsewhere, in the placement of the figure in the space Katz can accomplish a very abstract sense of verticality or horizontality, juxtaposing the frequently vivid or off-beat color relationships with this cool, rather Platonic compositional soundness. I should also mention the occasional humor of this work, particularly in the "Arrow Shirt" series and the "Hat" series, which gives his compositional distinctiveness a certain lightness (Look ma, no hands!) and subtlety. I guess I've mentioned every *possible* quality by now, but there it is.

One of the most beautiful moments in 20th century painting, the moment of Arshile Gorky, has been memorialized in two exhibitions this season: *Paintings from 1929 to 1948* at the Sidney Janis Gallery and *Drawings from 1929 to 1934* at the David Anderson Gallery. I say moment, I suppose, because this artist's work now seems to spring from a single impulse, the impulse to be *studiously marvelous,* though in actuality the work amounts probably to a century. There are few disappointing Gorkys, and no uninteresting ones. His range was tremendous, his stance singular and unified. As early as 1930 or so (the painting is dated "circa") he had created a masterpiece, the *Portrait of Master Bill* (de Kooning), and it was not to be his last. Already he had discovered a method of both modeling the figure and flattening the modeled forms which were to be forgotten during the "cubist" phase and to be rediscovered in the last works, and the head has the intriguing reminiscence of Coptic art and Roman wall painting which also appears in the *Self Portrait* (c. 1937) and the Whitney Museum's great *Portrait of the Artist as a Boy, with his Mother*

(c. 1930-39). What Gorky went on to is, of course, one of the most extra-ordinary revelations of sensibility in our time.

The two exhibitions complemented each other admirably. In the Janis Gallery one saw the "cream of the crop" paintings, early, middle (with their Picasso and Miró influences) and last. At David Anderson there was yet another early masterpiece, *Nighttime, Enigma and Nostalgia* (c. 1929-34), a prophetic abstraction, flanked by numerous drawings, many of them variants of the painting's theme, providing a welcome opportunity to study Gorky's tenacious elaboration of theme and motif and his very de-liberative technique of summoning his unconscious to the surface. But I don't mean that these drawings were just for study. Their very eclecticism (from Picasso to de Chirico) gave one that strange exhilaration about art (with capital letters, glamor and history all thrown in) which only a master can give, and does give at every period of his work.

Back at the Janis Gallery, his gift was celebrated handsomely. One may have many Gorkys, depending on the selection, and this exhibition pre-sented a different aspect of the painter. Mr. Janis is to be praised for this discriminating service in 1953, 1955, 1957, 1959 and 1962, each exhibi-tion delineating another aspect of Gorky's genius, each an experience for which one must be humbly grateful. The exhibition this year presented a less "characteristic" Gorky. We were not so much involved with his sinuous and mysterious line and with floral-phallic imagery as with mass and flux, with formal ambiguities solved by decisions of sensibility both rational and erudite. One saw Gorky's heroes in the *Still Life* (c. 1929) (Cézanne), *Organization* (c. 1932) (Picasso) and *To My Maro* (1946) (Miró), but the line of his achievement was inevitable and strong, and his personal strength as an artist was presented in the sunlight, so to speak, with a clarity and solidity and logic which did not deny, but rather ampli-fied the sensuality characteristic of his abstract work of the 1940s. In the ambiance of the early works, which are "covered" in a way with personal-ity, it was particularly gratifying to see the nude limpidity of *Untitled* (1943-48), *Terra Cotta* (1947) and *Last Painting* (1948.) One does not go naked unless one is strong. They too are masterpieces, and have given the direction to several styles of current painting. Everything wasn't in-vented by Kandinsky.

This month also sees the publication of Harold Rosenberg's *Arshile Gorky*, a brilliant monograph on the artist, his work and his position in modern art which is recommended to all. Mr. Rosenberg is that rarest of things, the right man in the right place at the right time. What more could one ask for? Taken with Thomas B. Hess's *Willem de Kooning* as partner, we now have the most lucid and informed explication to date, not just of these two individual artists, but of the general developments and problems of contemporary American painting. Both writers raise as many questions as they answer, and the books are therefore expansive as well as definitive. Mr. Rosenberg's book, among the appendices, includes André Breton's beautiful farewell poem to his friend. Everything that Gorky touched, and everything that touched him, seems from this untragic distace to have been beautiful.

[*Kulchur* II:6, Summer 1962]

ART CHRONICLE III

The Modern Museum opened its new season with a full-fledged retro-
spective of Mark Tobey, which is to say there were slightly under one
hundred and fifty works. Tobey, if we are to believe our European com-
patriots, is the most important American artist living today: he was the
first American artist since Whistler to be awarded the grand international
prize for painting at the Venice Biennale a few years ago and the first
American artist to have a large one-man show in the Louvre (over three
hundred works this time) a couple of years later. He is not as important
as the Europeans think, any more than Klee or Wols is, but he has done im-
portant work and it was all in the Museum of Modern Art. Then why was
his exhibition such a disappointment?

For one thing, we look upon the retrospective of a respected artist
with a kind of endless expectation: it will be a summation, a vindication,
an apotheosis. It never happens. There are good shows and bad shows.
Major artists have no need for retrospectives, they are simply an aid to
more easily assimilated information about known excellences. I should
have far preferred that only the most exquisite Tobeys, whether or not
they represented the artist's interests from period to period, be shown:
Tobey is wonderfully exquisite, and when he is not exquisite he is not
wonderful.

But what is the difference in our taste and that of the European art-
lovers? First of all we are not art-lovers, not precisely that. If one were to
characterize perhaps the greatest collection of modern American abstract
art, that of Mr. and Mrs. Ben Heller, one would hardly say that it was one
of art-lovers. It is more pragmatic than that: it is a collection of tested,
and tried, and therefore true value. By "therefore" I mean difficulty of
process, not inevitability. The fault in this exhibition is that it was chosen
with an eye to making Tobey a major artist in his own land, to document
his humanism, his technical exploration, his compositional variety, his
spirituality. Tobey has done fine things in his own way, on his own time,
but they will never be major, any more than Redon will ever challenge
Renoir. Tobey is the Clara Haskill of painting, not the Arthur Schnabel.
He is neither as important as Mr. Seitz thinks (in his catalog to the exhi-
bition) nor as despicable as Mr. Kramer thinks (in his review in *The
Nation*, which is almost a review of the catalog, instead of the paintings),
he is a very fine artist. The solution to his European adulation is very

simple: there is a New York School because there is an open-eyed New York public, just as there was an École de Paris because there was an open-eyed Parisian public. Decadence lowers the lids. New York's (for how long, oh Lord?) have not yet been lowered. Until they are, we shall have wide and powerful affinities (Rembrandt's *The Polish Rider* and Pollock's *Autumn Rhythm*), and suffering young artists assailing the barricades and getting one or two vivas for their efforts, but we shall not yet have a *l'heure exquise* during which Fragonard seems more "honest" than Michelangelo. Not while Willem de Kooning and Barnett Newman are about. And while they are, Mr. Tobey must keep his place, as he has in the past, not an ignoble position, but rather a chosen one. As Delacroix said, "Delicacy of feeling does not preclude major emotions in Cimarosa." But the major emotions which have been instilled in us by twenty years of great American painting cannot be wiped away so soon by either the West Coast, Japan (Zen) or Europe. In the light of "abstract-expressionism," which did indeed change the history of art, Zen is merely common-sense, and European esthetics just sophistication. With these artists a new grandeur, breadth and candor entered the forms of art, a necessary quality, as necessary for its time as Lautrec's or Rembrandt's for theirs, and one cannot go back, except in time.

   Candor, which of course has its own built-in breadth and grandeur, is the dominant quality in Claes Oldenburg's new work at the Green Gallery, and he has an ironic and sometimes hilarious sense of paradox to drive his points home. Where most of the other artists grouped by opinion into the "new realist" or "pop art" movement tend to make their art *out of* vulgar (in the sense of everyday) objects, images and emblems, Oldenburg makes the very objects and symbols themselves, with the help of papier-mâché, cloth, wood, glue, paint and whatever other mysterious materials are inside and on them, *into* art. His was one of the most amusing, cheering and thought-provoking exhibitions this year. Beautifully modeled and painted bacon-and-eggs or slices of pie on real (old) kitchen plates, on low pedestals, led one towards a monumental pair of work pants on a hanger and another over a chair, each heavier-looking than bronze, and just beyond them a seven-foot pistachio ice cream cone (painted cloth) lay on the floor, flanked by a monstrous wedge of chocolate and vanilla layer cake of the same materials and scale and a hamburger (with pickle round on top) which, if used as an ottoman, could sit at least twenty fairly large persons. The juxtapostions of scale in the show, the use of "real" plates, kitchen utensils, chairs and commercial display cases of chrome and glass (pie racks, etc.)

in conjunction with the created "food," each executed with an acute
esthetic attention to shape, texture and variety of color, were bewildering
in the very best sense, causing one to halt (an unusual occurence in New
York except at intersections), and appreciate. With the perverse charms
of Gulliver and of Alice-in-Wonderland, Oldenburg makes one feel almost
hysterically present, alert, summoned to the party. There is no hint of
mysticism, no "significance," no commentary, in the work. He is like a
Fabergé in love with Broadway, or a Pollock who has just read the Cordon
Bleu Cookbook (in American). Oddly enough, since it is really I suppose
sculpture, his work relates somewhat to Pollock's cutout painting of the
late 40s. I recall in particular a cutout wooden figure by Pollock, shaped
rather like a cloverleaf and painted in his drip technique and done to be
hung free from a wire; Oldenburg has a comic edge and whimsy like that
figure, but I doubt if he could have ever seen it since it disappeared around
1952 and has never been recovered, and so far as I know there were no
other Pollock "sculptures" of this kind, I bring him up only to indicate
how much of the pleasure and brilliance of painting is in Oldenburg's work,
whether brushed or dripped on the strange preoccupations of his mind. It
may be too that part of Oldenburg's vivacity consists in the satiric employ-
ment of "delicious" abstract paint-techniques to render our delicious des-
serts and snacks and in the suave monumentalizing (his huge cloth pieces
have zippers) of contemporary American Bread and Wine and Pants, but
I think there is more to it all than that. At any rate there is nothing chichi
or wall-eyed in his work, an unusually positive quality for an artist work-
ing in this general tendency to have right now.

    In the other corner of the "constructed commonplace" movement, or I
should probably say reconstructed if it didn't smack of 1867 (which it
may actually resemble more than anything else) in the Deep South, paces
Niki de St. Phalle, armed with a gun. It is not the ray-gun of New York,
with its humorous-Nihilistic overtones and Pogoesque sarcasm, but a gun
with which to shoot into bags of pigment and thus "enter" the work as
a participant in its composition as you hit a sac of pigment and thus effect
an alteration in the picture. What hath Pollock wrought? you don't even
have to put the thing on the floor any more and you can even get some-
one else to finish it, as a boyfriend helps his girlfriend win a panda at Pal-
isades Park. Where Oldenburg contains his personality Miss de St. Phalle
encourages the ruination of hers (as an artist), a provocative and endearing
position. The whole atmosphere is very European; it is as if she had em-
braced a great many Western movies and through utter sincerity made the

method of them her own. Where it is not that, there is a very complete concentration on religious creepiness, fetishism and organic decay. Her shrines, compounded of dolls, plaster, cloth and slopped paint, resurrect a confectioner's nightmare of his first view of the Grunewald Altarpiece and elsewhere in the more objective pieces it is not long before you, by your own hand and aim, have caused blood or pus to flow. I say European because there is a very strong and rather repulsive logic behind it all, it is certainly iconographic in intent, if not conviction, and probably mystic. It is also, like *parfum*, attractive and disturbing and frequently repellent: if you are before a decomposing shrine it is you, not the God, that's decomposing; if you shoot and burst a condom full of paint, is that paint just paint or is it the penis within? It is actually very interesting, and if this whole tendency has been referred to with some justice as *sale morbidité*, it is not so *sale* as all that, and it represents an attitude towards destruction which is not without a great deal more justification by objective reality than most people working in the New Realism — if I am right in thinking that they are all children of Hieronymus Bosch, Miss de St. Phalle is way ahead of the field. And I'm glad I'm not lying in that field looking for four-leaf clovers. But at least she is not dallying with a Magritte idea of a billboard or a Léger interpretation of a comic strip, or a mid-Western Forest Ranger's gimmick for stopping a car most economically (for his respective state), or a Madison Avenue luncher's appetite for being yummy from a can. I guess she really *is* religious..

Abstract-expressionism, which has been dying in the daily and weekly press for lo! these many months, has also been abandoned in her recent show by Grace Hartigan, a motion self-proclaimed in her catalog preface. In the largest painting, *The The,* she showed a continuance of the very ambitious figurative-abstract-expressionist expression through which she achieved considerable renown for her own "Second Generation" interpretation of the New York School style; it is a somewhat botched-up painting, but admirable in its ambitiousness and adamancy. Elsewhere, save for *The Dream,* a very interesting move towards a more subtle Matisse-ish arabesque line and more modulated palette, her defection has produced little but repetitiousness of feeling, and in at least two pictures, *Marilyn Monroe* and *Clark's Cove,* a vulgarity of spirit which is quite disheartening in that it employs illusionistic devices to further apparently unfelt ends. Strangely enough, Miss Hartigan even in her most expressionist moments of the past has never seemed more German — her Monroe here is a movie star as seen by Kirchner *cum* Jack Levine. But she has done remarkable and important

work in the past and will, I'm sure, in the future; it may be, as Pasternak
said of the early Mayakovsky, that her new pose does not yet fit her tal-
ents, that she has not yet become her pose. This is not meant in a deprecat-
ing sense, but rather in a realistic one. The techniques by which an artist
keeps going are not confined to the materials of the studio.

HOWEVER, Allen Stone, for the opening of his new gallery on 86th
Street, has assembled the best show so far this season, one of the best in
many seasons, a testament to the superb distinction of two contemporary
masters ranging over the past twenty years: a show of works by Willem de
Kooning and Barnett Newman. In close juxtaposition, each artist remained
even more totally individual in content and style than one would have im-
agined, considering that they are both labelled abstract-expressionist, and
their works took on a relaxed brilliance, an easy mastery, as if the paint-
ings were discussing with each other some profound problem of style which
had already been solved to different, but mutual, satisfactions. Mr. Stone
assembled some of the most important paintings by each artist, an em-
barrassment of riches many of which had been known to the public only in
black and white reproduction, and an event of such importance that, on the
nether side, it should have embarrassed most of the museums in the vicinity.
There were also recent works by each artist: if Mr. Canaday and Miss
Genauer want to think that abstract-expressionism is dead I hope they both
kept looking at the moribund art they've been looking at all along and
stayed away from this show.

Most of the attention of these two critics recently has been diverted from
actual works of art to polemical dissertation on art's tangential appurte-
nances, collecting and marketing. Many the feeble-minded exposé that has
greeted one's eyes, hardly any praise that isn't aimed at ruining some other
artist's reputation, hardly ever a deviation from the neurotic assertion that
no artist, however great, can ever wholly take in the omnipotent *Times*
and *Trib.* Take them in where? With their esthetic chastity belts hitched
so tight, there has never been much reason why either one of them ever
ventured forth to a gallery. And each has devoted, at least one slack week
in each season, a whole column to their difficulties in getting themselves
physically to the galleries, Mr. Canaday notably in his lament over bus
service on Madison Avenue column, and Miss Genauer in her candid ap-
praisal of a safari as far south as Houston Street, with aid of cab driver and
delicatessen clerk, in search of the Delancey Street Museum. Neither one
of them has any better sense of geography or traffic than they do of art.

Mr. Canaday's specialty along this line has been the wise-suspicion-of-esthetic-hoax strategy, a strategy aimed exclusively at the abstract-expressionists with the equally simplistic belief, apparently, that no figurative artist has ever wanted to sell a painting. It was especially amusing in the light of this to read the two columns in which he first praised the Chrysler Collection for its service in showing atypical paintings by modern masters, and later the one in which he was forced to announce that these very paintings had been exposed as fakes by a committee of art experts, gracefully attributing his previous enthusiasm to an excellent lobster lunch and the heat of the summer sun in Provincetown, Massachusetts, where the Chrysler Museum is located. In the one where Mr. Canaday had the opportunity to inform the public of an actual artistic fraud he was asleep at the switch he has so frequently raised in the *Times* against the conniving museums, galleries, collectors and distinguished contemporary artists who, he has frequently alleged, are united to bilk the gullible for financial gain. Of course everyone makes mistakes, I go into this matter at such length only because Mr. Canaday had been punishing his betters for some time now from the vantage point of a scholarly perspective; yet when he sees a portrait of a woman in the current style of Washington Square Expressionism *signed* as a van Gogh, or a sketch of a nude which might be barely *attributed* to Othon Friesz *labelled* Matisse, or a still life most typical of certain American followers of Soutine in the mid-50s *presented* as a Bonnard (!), our critic's historical perspective (including the recent extensive documentation of fakes of all periods) dwindles to the size of a Chrysler hubcap and the ears of the watchdog so alert to "phoniness" in abstract art collapse in the midday sun for all the world like Lassie straying onto the set of Noel Coward's sincere and beautiful musical *Sailaway* during a performance. Mr. Chrysler must give wonderful lunches. Mr. Canaday, who has often opined that critics who hobnob with *artists* are in danger of losing their critical objectivity, must be a wonderful luncheon guest, whether he ever really had that lunch or not. At any rate, Mr. Canaday, whether admiring "atypical examples" (*sic*) of famous painters, or attacking abstract painters, or pushing the Hiroshima-Humanist works he finds so significant, has definitely proven that he does not care to discriminate between an ugly work and a beautiful one. He is only interested in social credentials (no wonder the existentialists are at least more interesting than the humanists), and if that hideous "van Gogh" portrait could be proven to be a Picasso spoof on van Gogh's sunflower period he would probably recommend it highly. There are plenty of falsely attributed paintings of all periods hung around the world, but the false

attribution is usually a labored and stylistically documented compliment
to the qualities of the artist or school being imitated. The recently exposed
fake Etruscan sculptures in the Metropolitan Museum are still eminently
worth studying, and if as some French gossip has it the Museum of Modern
Art's Rousseau *The Sleeping Gypsy* was actually painted by Derain, it is
still a masterpiece. The scandal about the Chrysler Collection is consider-
ably more confusing and ambiguous: for what (cynical?) reasons would a
collector who has had the taste and sagacity to purchase several indisput-
able masterpieces wish to present works whose attribution can only re-
duce our idea of the accomplishment of the artist in question? At present
writing this question is under consideration by the Canadian Parliament,
since a major Canadian museum lent its auspices to the second showing
of the exhibition.

Another private collection, which in numbers rivals many a public one,
the Joseph H. Hirshhorn Collection, has appeared under the auspices of
the Guggenheim Museum and is a marvel to behold. The Guggenheim shows
only sculpture from the collection, and it is inclusive and gregarious in
nature, but among the over four hundred works displayed, given the weak-
ness of the David Smith selection, and the overemphasis on Manzù,
an Italian sculptor who has finally driven the last note of glamor out of
the word "Mannerism," one finds superb examples of major sculptors,
surprisingly fine examples by minor ones, pieces by Bourdelle which are
enough in themselves to cause a re-evaluation of his work, and groups of
works by Rodin, Brancusi, Degas and Daumier, which should be the crown
jewels of any collection. The Henry Moores are an exemplary collection
too, but next to the Daumiers they seem caught in some frostbitten, monu-
mental lethargy which is sometimes referred to as the English Channel. But
then I prefer the Viennese-bronze-caricature *sense* of Daumier to the mono-
lithic platitudes of Moore every time, so I may be wrong.

The Iolas Gallery this season, where Miss de St. Phalle showed, has of-
fered three other New-Realists (European Branch): Jean Tinguely, Mar-
tial Raysse and the late Yves Klein.

Yves Klien died this summer in his mid-thirties. He was a genius in the
old-fashioned sense of the word: he was brilliant, like a meteorite, or, to
some like a firecracker (remembering that the firecracker is one of the
most beautiful and ephemeral of human inventions), and he used the
properties of both in his work when he made his "burnt-sea" sculptures,
his flame-paintings, and his fountains of colored water and ignited jets
of gas through which the wind could force its remolding, recombining will.

Through one of those odd ironies his death was presaged by a note of condolences sent to his Paris dealer mistakenly by an admirer who had read of the death of Franz Kline, and a very few weeks later the condolences were apt. It was an incident not at all out of keeping with the phenomenal and Romantic career of Klein: admiring Kline, he thought the note was flattering, it appealed to his latent Byronism. Yves Klein was a unique person in contemporary art: his sensibility continually outsmarted his ingenuity, and his ingenuity outsmarted his adversaries (of which he had many). The Iolas exhibition could not, under the circumstances, present him in the way he should have been presented in New York, as his previous show at Castelli did not, but it gave a greater sense of his genuine gift than anyone has seen here before. The *monochrome-bleu* paintings were wonderful, there were no major fire-paintings available, and the sponge works were too sparse. Still, the effort to honor him was noble, and the catalog, with Klein's own superb esthetic dialectic presented so well, somehow filled in the gaps. Perhaps not for a non-enthusiast, but I don't care about them. His work has an intellectual lucidity, a personal face-to-faceness and a sensuality which is nowhere else apparent in the new realists.

Jean Tinguely, of course, has little if anything to do with the new realists except for his inclusion in the Janis Gallery show of the group. He, like Klein, has given them some important impetus but, like Agostini, he seems apart from the show by his superiority. It's odd that artists equally eligible, and equally peripheral, like Robert Rauschenberg, Larry Rivers, Jasper Johns, Alex Katz, and for that matter César, were also not included. Tinguely's distinction was indomitable, however: in the gallery section his radio piece was masterful, a really unusually graceful contemporary work, right up there with Duchamp and Picabia, and in the store section his frigidaire was the most startingly amusing entry in a show which did not refrain from straining to be amusing. Since almost everyone in the two-department Janis show of new realists showed works based on the abstract-expressionist schema as individualized (for *them*), or satirized, into an available mode of feeling for expression, it may be interesting to point out that the best works were those in which the connections between the originator of the idea, the off-shooter and the new-realizer were most clear. Art, these days, is everything, including Life, and these were also the best artist in the show: Oldenburg (Gaudi and Miró through Pollock), Dine (Barnett Newman through Jasper Johns and Bob Rauschenberg), Segal (Giacometti through Larry Rivers' sculptures of the late 50s), Rosenquist (Magritte through Motherwell).

Martial Raysse was one of the very few Europeans among the new realists (and the movement was, after all, invented in Paris – here it came out of pop art and happenings originally with entirely different causes and effects) who did not slump in contrast to the American artists' works. He has a peculiar deftness, his work is melancholy and empty and funny and nasty; he has a way with color, with objects and with textures which the more chichi American new realists seem to be mincing towards but can't quite reach. He is the real thing in the extremely limited field of operations he has set himself, far more "real," for instance, than Spoerri, who keeps diaries of why he did what to which object because of whose arrival and remarks and actions during the constructions of his assemblages, etc. That is, Raysse's work has an esthetic reality and immediacy, where Spoerri's has a kind of cozy wisdom, as when you read that Gertrude Stein's portrait of T. S. Eliot was like that because Alice B. Toklas was sewing when he made his visit. *Raysse Beach* (which I hope was an intentional homage to Jacob Riis Park's beach), as presented at the Iolas Gallery, with its juke box, bathing beauty photographs, rubber toys and pool and sand, was marvelous in the international sense, though French to the toes. Where an American "new realist" like Andy Warhol loses the point of his new medium and makes a painting of a diagram of a dance step and then places a keep-off sign in front of it, Raysse's beaches are to be inhabited and played with, and when Raysse tints or paints a blown-up photograph it becomes more, not less, alluring. If the beach is any example, some enterprising gallery or museum should persuade Raysse to recreate one of his notorious supermarkets in New York. He is said to have found the ones existing here already very disappointing.

Which brings up a basic difference between the two elements so falsely joined in the Janis show. If group there be, there certainly must be two: *Nouvelle Réalisme* is a European invention or group, and the Americans may be more clarifyingly, though no less inaccurately, called Pop Art. The names have already been assigned, however muddledly. They have a rather vague truth by inference: the European artists so designated do indeed find the surprising more ordinary than the mundane, the fortuitous more causal than the deliberate, the accidental more understandable than the planned. For the American "pop artists" the struggle into existentiality seems more difficult: though the work is frequently far better in quality, it is also far less gracious, and it has often a numbing smugness and cracker-barrel cheerfulness, stemming often I suspect from European precendents which the Eurpoeans themselves have long since found old hat, from a "smart" interpretation of Marcel Duchamp's "silence" (*sic*) and of Miró's "camp." At their worst the Americans of this tendency act like Mark Twain trying to design a chess set. But it is an understandable reaction to the austere dialectical imperatives of abstract-expressionism and presents these artists with an open esthetic field of operations. And at their best, the Americans prove anew what Picasso and Joseph Cornell (to name only two artists especially pertinent to the "movement") have so often shown us: that there is no aspect (or for that matter artifact) of modern life which can *not* become art.

William Seitz, who earlier in the season organized the Tobey exhibition, has recently given us a very great show of paintings, studies and drawings by Arshile Gorky at the Museum of Modern Art. Following the Gorky shows mentioned in a previous issue, this is a large, eloquent and authoritative presentation of the work of one of the most important painters of our time. Most of the major works have not been seen together in New York since the Whitney Museum's exhibition in 1949; their conjunction can only impress one anew with the convicition of Gorky's greatness. The selection of the less important works, the early paintings, the studies and the drawings, is so judicious and so sensitive, that the effect of the exhibition is an amplification and enrichening of the major works and of Gorky's genius. In the wealth of achievement which this exhibition sets forth, Gorky's influences seem less pertinent, even in the early works, and his sensibility, that marvelously aristocratic mind and eye, compounded of Near-Eastern subtlety and American adventurousness, assumes its proper position as a major and original event in our culture. Gorky had a tremendous range of esthetic tradition to inspire and aid him and he used it in a passionate, individual way. In the exhibition at the Modern, the installation is simple and adroit: the elaborations of forms in the series, the relationships of studies to paintings and to their motival offshoots, the linking of opposing tendencies in Gorky's development, all these qualities are so well understood and felt in the hanging that the works come to you clear and decisive and powerful. Of course all this is Gorky, which is the highest praise an exhibition can have, to serve well the complicated interests of its subject.

Three other shows not unrelated to Gorky, were those of Al Held (Poindexter Gallery), Robert Motherwell (Janis) and Larry Rivers (Tibor de Nagy) — they have each been involved in the best of recent tradition and in the search for their own interpretation of it, as was Gorky, and they are each involved in contemporary High Art which, gossip to the contrary, has never stopped being more exciting than pop art (chiefly I suppose because

it is more difficult to achieve). At any rate I mention them because of the
very high quality of the shows, not for any tie-in with Gorky, except in
two peripheral instances, which is to say that I believe Held has taken up
a very beautiful motion of Gorky's late 30s, just when Gorky was moving
into a "hard" forceful style which he soon abandoned, and Held has forged
from this brief insight a grand, capacious expressive instrument. Rivers has
been influenced, in a similarly "off" way, by certain minor characteristics
of Gorky's draughtsmanship and coloring. It is not an influence concentra-
ted in any one aspect of Gorky, or in any one period of Rivers, but rather
as if the earlier artist had confided some secrets of the eye, finger and
wrist which, after Rivers' last studiously overt figurative works of 1953,
have never left his consciousness. Unless my own eye is mistaken, Gorky's
example can be discerned in many felicities of Rivers' addition-subtraction
method of delineating in his drawing, and in his perfect placement of seem-
ingly unrelated passages of color in order to strengthen the total pictorial
image – though he is most often thought of as a figurative or semi-figura-
tive painter, this usage in Rivers' work points toward a more abstract feel-
ing for the picture-plane than is found in many a neo-plasticist. It is, for
instance, very clear in the present show's drawings and collages that the
anatomical pieces are abstract compilations of figurative parts in which
Composition is All. The totaliy of these small works is not the aggregate
of sensitively drawn fragments and details, though Rivers is one of the
finest draughtsmen in America, but the sum of a totally felt pictorial
conception. The oils in Rivers' show have a strong totality too: the franc
notes, the Camel packs and the nudes with vocabulary lessons stenciled
next to the appropriate parts of the body are not unlike the "psychological-
map" aspect of Gorky's late paintings, where the act of painting, and the
finished painting itself, seem to bloom through some extra concern of the
artist which is "other" than the making of a good or grand painting. In
this respect, and in his pursuit of whatever the handling of the paint leads
towards, Rivers is far removed from Pop Artists who create ostensibly
similar images. Rivers is after a more complicated and mysterious visual
experience, more related to Johns and Rauschenberg than to Indiana and
Warhol. For Rivers the stencil is simply another element available to the
expression, to several other painters recently it has been *the* expression.
The latter idea is perfectly agreeable in theory, but the resultant works
have seldom gone further than the mechanics of their construction.

    In this connection Motherwell's series of Spanish Elegies continues to
expand and move. While the original image was discovered subconsciously,

by now it may be considered as preconceived in the later developments. Some preconceptions in imagery stand still at their freshest (soup cans, newspaper pages, road signs), like a high school performance of *The Petrified Forest*. But the Elegies mean something, and you can't beat that. Elsewhere in his show Motherwell has what one might have assumed from previous works, a great lyric gift. One of his titles, the largest painting in the show and one of his best, pretty much indicates his qualities as a painter: *The Golden Fleece*. His painting is most often embarked upon esthetic voyages, and he seldom returns without the treasure, here most notably in *Chi Ama, Crede*, the *Elegy to the Spanish Republic No. 70* and *No. 77*, and the new series of *Beside the Sea* paintings, with their brilliant calligraphic splashes leaping up from deep horizontal bands of paint.

Also among the most important new works of this season were Al Held's abstract paintings at the Poindexter Gallery. Huge in format for the most part, they are thickly and smoothly painted, building up strongly colored shapes in juxtaposition to each other and to the positive or negative relation of the plane. It is difficult to convey the strange qualities Held is able to achieve simultaneously: monumentality and wit, brassily strident relationships of color with sudden unobtrusive delicacies of detail, grandeur of stance emerging through deliberately off-kilter formal devices, humorously primary forms and colors adding up to symphonic complexity. Seen in group shows in the last few years, Held's work has looked increasingly more important and with this show following up his last one he has become one of the most controversial and powerful painters in New York.

[*Kulchur* III:9, Spring 1963]

RIOPELLE: INTERNATIONAL SPEEDSCAPES

"There is no figuration, there is only expression — and expression is just someone in front of things. . .

"The artist who has an ideology! — that's worse than having a system! It has sense for him, and has no sense for anyone else. . .

"Sensibility is your correspondence with your feeling for nature — complete nature, including your nature, your painting and yourself. There is only one reference: nature. . .

"There is no time that is *not* your own time, that you can *not* do what you must do. . . There is no color more colorful than black and white if that is what you do in your own time. . . You don't paint for nothing, you paint for yourself, that is your satisfaction, that is what makes you do what you do with and for your own time: there is only yourself, and the past, and what you do. . .

"I prefer the chapel of Matisse [at Vence] to any in the world because, according to my ideal, he would have done the same thing for a whorehouse."

Jean-Paul Riopelle enjoys the double distinction of being one of the most important figures to emerge in the School of Paris since the end of World War II and probably the most important artist in Canada's history. The remarks quoted above come from a recent conversation which included references to the painter's admiration for Ruysdael, Courbet, Paulus Potter, the Corot *Italiennes*, Vuillard, Sam Francis and, as one might suspect from one of the quotes, Franz Kline, of whom he also said, "Kline was a great painter and a great figure, so how can anyone prefer anyone to him?"

Two years ago in Paris he had also expressed this rather exclusive admiration for Kline, remarking then that the originality of his space was singular in that it was uniquely independent of landscape or still-life conventions, concluding that, "once he painted abstract he gave us a *new* space. The space of his personal."

The "personal" stuck in my mind because it is characteristic of Riopelle to be almost totally uninterested in nouns — he finds specific qualities important and assumes that you perfectly well know what the object of that importance is; Riopelle's own work shares only this quality of personalness-in-the-space with Kline's, nothing more. Even with artists whose aims would seem generally closer, this is true: his space and his gesture are as unrelated to Pollock's or de Kooning's as they are to Fautrier's or Soulages'. And I don't think this has anything to do with boyhood memories. While European critics have often gone into paeans of praise for his presenting to Paris, Düsseldorf or Basel, *enfin et au fond*, the very spirit and essence of the Great Canadian Forest, it is difficult to find this actuality visually present in his work, unless one can imagine oneself the bandit in *Rashomon* looking at a Riopelle on the ceiling. The nature to which his conversation frequently adheres is at its most specific a kind of pantheistic rationalization designed to guard his love affair with art, evolved from his passion over art's expressive possibilities. From the developments of his own work he would be forced to agree with Goethe — "A work of art is just as much a work of nature as a mountain." The Romantics found that the expressivity of which art was capable became too large to be confined by rationalist terminology and a new metaphor was sought to indicate its breadth and power. The same is true today, now that the dominant rationalism of cubist order has been broken through. Being essentially mysterious, "nature," where it does not imply naturalism, is the least misleading metaphor for this changed situation.

What Riopelle, in his work, does evoke of nature is the thoroughness and completeness with which spontaneous energies seek and achieve their aims and the unendingness of the process which bears the forces of continuation. There is completion, but no contemplation, in his pictures; stylistic instinct, but not stylistic logic. He has technically at his service a prodigiously accomplished finesse, and his hand and eye are capable of great delicacy and exquisite organization (particularly in the watercolors, which relate to Watteau as well as Masson), but all this is serving an almost brutal lyricism, headstrong, impetuous and carnal. The space which the lyricism explores (in the oils) is layed on, ducked into, tucked up, with brush, spatula and knife to spread forth one large field of image which is setting free a thousand minute ones. In general, because of the modernity of Riopelle's sensibility the landscape aura is less a matter of spiritual evocation (which is itself generalized, rather than specific) than of speed, with its built-in anxiety for swift preception. Where the painting most closely relates to landscape, it is a landscape abstracted by a quick, close look at its essentials, as if seen from a jet plane or a speeding sports car. (Riopelle's relaxations from painting and sculpture are sailing, fishing and racing sports cars; he was a flier in World War II.) If a landscape seems there at all, one is rushing through it, grabbing its most salient aspects as it goes by, or drowning in it and giving it the forced attention one would give to the Straw.

Riopelle admires, above all, painting which is *habile* — adroit, instictive in

its use of the medium, finding its inspiration in it, rather than on it or
through it. In his search for the qualities of his mediums he has been at times
a figurative painter (before 1945), an automatist, a tachist, an abstract-
expressionist; as a Canadian painter in Paris, his researches seem to have
more closely parallelled those of the Americans than those of other mem-
bers of the School of Paris. Like the Americans, he was influenced by sur-
realism in a special, non-literal way (and appreciated by the surrealists: his
1949 catalogue was written by Benjamin Péret, André Breton and the latter's
then wife). He was also deeply dissatisfied with the European well-planned
picture which was inching its way from cubism to a nerveless future. By 1950
he was already presenting to Paris a vision which had broken free from auto-
matism and surrealist influences, and which was to remain unaccompanied in
quality until Jackson Pollock was exhibited there in 1952. (I omit Mathieu
here, for one, because the effort was so totally dissimilar.)

In the following year Riopelle's style changed rapidly from the richly elab-
orated and skeined "controlled drip" technique, with its dense surfaces
whipped and trailed over by strings of impasto, to an equally dense surface
over which the impasto was pushed and stroked with a knife: the paintings
increased in scale, in vividness of color juxtapositions and in solidity of struc-
ture. These were the paintings that first made him famous and to which the
phrase "mosaic style" was attached, though it gives no very accurate sense of
the look. For, paradoxically, this intricate and laborful technique, with its
seemingly infinite opportunities for control and adjustment (as compared to
the previously impetuous floods and dashes of paint), gave rise to some of
his most violent and declamatory works. And this more intellectual and more
formal period, which has been described as having both architectural and
sculptural "values" in the abstract sense of the words, was at the same time
capable of being interpreted quite literally, through ambiguities of luminosity
and of surface effects, as a period of blizzards and butterflies.

Throughout his work Riopelle is spontaneous, illuminatory and quick; to
varying degrees, but these qualities are always there. Along with them goes
a certain toughness and hardness: nothing is going to look easy, nothing is
going to be pretty. Except in some of the smaller watercolors and colored
inks, there is usually a severity of structure and heaviness of form underlying
the fireworks which, like a barely conscious compulsion, gives the sometimes
rather hedonistic effects of the paint-handling their ambiguous strength and
drama.

It is precisely this dramatic ambiguity which inhabits the sculptures
Riopelle has done in the last two years. While bearing no specific relation to

his painting, their surfaces are rich and sensuous — done in the lost-wax process, they are very "handled" — but one suspects that some carnivorous flower or monster may be lurking within. (As a painter doing sculptures, it may be interesting to note, he insists on the wax so that the forms can be handled as directly and sensitively as he wishes.)

The paintings in the last few years have moved towards a more open vision. The brush has returned and with it greater variety of impasto, and larger forms and expanses emerge more by their own volition, seemingly, than as accumulations of multitudinous paint-events. In some there is more centralization of mass, less concern for an all-over image, and the tension established between the mass and non-mass has a new resonance. Paintings such as *The Dance* and *The Queen of Spades* to me are grander, more varied in their plastic ambitions and more powerful than ever before. At thirty-nine, Riopelle is on the heights of an extraordinary career which may well dwell in that spiritual land of Pope's where "Alps on Alps arise."

[*Art News,* April 1963]

APOLLINAIRE'S PORNOGRAPHIC NOVELS

Unfortunately I don't have an extensive acquaintance with pornographic writing, but I have read everything I could. The novels that have seemed the best to me in this line are few: *Fanny Hill*, the two Apollinaire novels I want to discuss here (*Memoirs of a Young Rakehell* and *The Debauched Hospodar*), and *Candy*. Unlike much pornographic writing, they are very unlike each other in style and intent. *Fanny Hill* is a masterpiece which can only be discussed with other pornography because it simultaneously exploits this *genre* to perfection while maintaining a marvellous literary joy. *Candy* is a perverse, free-wheeling satire on the obscene which on the way enlarges that subject to include religion, social pretension, kindness and avarice, as well as intercourse, but its cracks at these foibles are so dirty (if you'll forgive me) that it safely comes to a religious, even mythical, conclusion without ever having veered off into straight satire. Unlike *Lolita*, it sticks to its guns, so to speak, by being amiable and sly.

Both Apollinaire novels, or more properly tales, are very peculiar. It is obviously irresistible to him to indulge in some finer points of style and perception, but these are managed so subtly and so unobtrusively that they never get "serious" — on the contrary, they contribute a mocking unselfconscious quality to the narrative which keeps it from getting leaden or sweaty, as most pornography must (or has). They keep Apollinaire's interest in the writing from flagging, and they keep the reader from becoming fatigued at the "recitation" which such works always fall into. I do not mean that either of these novels is a masterpiece, like *Fanny Hill*, but they are wonderful works and they reveal some interesting things about Apollinaire.*

The result of all this is that no one knows what pornography is any more. The square thinks everything in serious literature is, the hip thinks absolutely nothing can be or he'll be a traitor to himself. For the sake of going on, let's assume that pornography is again a work which is created solely to arouse the sexual passions, hardon-wise. It cannot have a serious literary attention. It must always be written for a small sum of desperately needed money. It must be indefensible to the postal authorities, even if it's a literary phenomenon (like *Fanny Hill*). It only rarely might be appealed under the category of delight (as the Apollinaire novels could, but

* Apparently a page is missing here. Ed.

so little else is delightful in this field), but Delight is hardly a serious postal category. Far from being an element of literature where the writer finds himself intimately engaged with his primal forces, pornography is the most difficult, limited, boring and laborious *genre* a writer could take on. And therefore it's an extremely interesting one. Personally, I wish the postal authorities would ban the detective novel, the autobiographical novel and the *roman à clef*, which, like the sonnet, are simple forms requiring only application, and let pornography run rampant. It, being something which requires great improvisatory skill, would undoubtedly yield some very interesting and [far] out results, but in the direction of literary invention, rather than psychological revelation.

Apollinaire approached the writing of pornography with a full barrage of literary ideas. It's quite obvious in the writing that he realized that the greatest problem is getting from lay to lay, and varying the lays sufficiently so that the reader can distinguish one from another. The human body having only a certain fixed number of organs and orifices, this is no small problem. Characteristically, Apollinaire pretty much waves it aside. Having probably the most original *attitude* toward events of any 20th century poet, Apollinaire nonchalantly commences each novel with a definite literary satire as the framework: *Memoirs of a Young Rakehell* starts as a spoof of the traditional French novel about "what happens to a boy who's just reached puberty during a summer in the family's country place" (and never has a boy had such a satisfactory summer, Colette or no Colette), and *The Debauched Hospodar* is a demented view of the Marquis de Sade's world told in the style of Jules Verne's *Michael Strogoff.* The one is an idyllic pastoral, the other a straightforward adventure story. As in his poems, the stance of Apollinaire is so strong that one finds oneself admiring the poet rather than the subject (as, for instance, compared with Frost or Yeats, which is why they're not modern). Each novel has a strong and interesting hero, a kind of Picaresque hero you enjoy identifying with, and everyone else is scenery. There is lots of geographical variety, too: in the *Memoirs* variety is achieved through the female members of the family and household (except for his mother, he *does* leave her alone, but he manages both sisters and an aunt), and in *Hospodar* the variety branches out to include both sexes, most races and creeds, and one dog. (The *Hospodar*, incidentally, gets himself involved in the Russo-Japanese War and the Siege of Port Arthur, which I somehow find very poignant.) Another identification-lure that both heroes have is that neither ever meets another male who could cause them the slightest genital envy. (*Aside:* Thinking

of Norman Brown's *Life Against Death*, most characters in pornographic
literature are very pleased with their genital orientation, perhaps because
they have no limit to their other sexual satisfactions because of it.)

But let me give you a sample of the nice wit with which Apollinaire
surrounds his young rake. The "novel" begins quietly with the family
(excepting the father, who is handily kept out of the way all but once as
possible competition) moving to the country. There is a little reminis-
cence of *Adolphe*, beginning with a rather malicious simplicity:

> "We arrived in the best of spirits at the country house, which the
> people of that district had nicknamed *Le Chateau*.
> "*Le Chateau*, which was an old dwelling no doubt dating from the
> 17th century, had once belonged to wealthy farmers."

Wasting no time, we are presently here:

> "Berthe was not wearing any panties, because, as she told me later,
> hers were dirty, and we had not yet had time to unpack the linen.
> "So it was that for the first time I saw my sister in an immodest
> state."

Of course immodesty is hardly the word for succeeding states involving
most of the characters in the novel, but there follows a brief and very
charming flashback in which our young hero, Roger, tells of his first intu-
itions of his own sexuality. These are largely involved with the matriarchal
arrangements for bathing young French males, and the tender care devoted
to all details by aunts and maidservants. France must have been a very
pleasant place, indeed, though when you think how boring it is to bathe
a child, and how aggravating it is when the child won't go to sleep, it's no
wonder that certain affectionate practices were indulged in which would
be generally frowned upon in New England.

Mony Vibescu, the Hereditary Hospodar and hero of the second novel,
is bisexual and therefore Apollinaire can pretty much quadruple the sexual
variety of incident. It is a far more panoramic work which takes a sort of
3-D Cinemascope approach to perversion, particularly the Sado-Masochistic,
while maintaining a terrible cheerfulness. Here, the poet of the "Chanson du
Mal-aimé" finds no holds are barred, and discovers a marvellous aplomb in
the idea that where you expect no love you encounter no sexual disappoint-
ment. The French title, *Onze mille verges* (a pun on *Onze mille vierges*), is

based on an allegedly folk saying to the sense that if you don't manage to deflower 11,000 virgins, you will get 11,000 lashes, a penalty for lack of initiative which would have made even Captain Bligh turn pale. Well, not to keep you in suspense, our hero does miss out by at least two or three conquests, though it must be admitted chiefly because he never met them. It is not *that* long a novel. He does his best, and no other court in the world would convict him.

The Debauched Hospodar begins, as does the *Rakehell*, with a lovely evocation of place, Bucharest in its decadence. Our hero in a chapter settles his affairs in his native city and departs for a Paris which is compounded of sex, violence and sadism: the City of Light.

THE SORROWS OF THE YOUNGMAN
JOHN RECHY'S *CITY OF NIGHT*

The prose of John Rechy is absolutely madly involved with adverbs. Also it is full of dots and dashes and elisions, à la Kerouac, and they frequently work well to create a run-on casual, or hysterical, faggotty diction which, along with the use of capitals for Emphasis of the important feeling-word (not always a noun as in German), gets marvelously accurately the Exact tone of homosexual bar-talk . . . which Is something, since I don't know of any other writer around recently who has managed this feat Unsquarely.

Well enough of that. *City of Night* comes to us with a great deal of anticipatory interest. Rechy's short prose pieces published in magazines have been widely admired by a steadily increasing public, and he has engaged the close attention of minds of considerable literary acumen: James Baldwin and Donald Allen, for two. Before publication, the novel was rumored to be a strong contender for the Prix Formentor, and since publication it has been distinguished by a panning in the *New York Review of Books* (representing the House of Lords) and a very cautious routine appraisal in the *New York Times* (representing the House of Commons). The Establishment is not with him, apparently, but nevertheless sales have been going well. Good.

City of Night is a dour picaresque novel with not much hu or in it and virtually no self-irony. The latter is fairly important to note since it is narrated in the first person, and the lack brings it closer to Thomas Wolfe than to Jean Genet, although the excerpts which had appeared previously seemed to indicate a Genetesque lyricism at work on America. (A friend of mine when asked about it said, "I like it, but why are gay novels always so sad?") Rechy's hero-narrator is a male hustler. He takes things very seriously, if not morbidly. He is not homosexual, to himself, although he betrays all the symptoms. He is a lonely (above all), deprived, curious Puritan adventurer who wants to know the worst about himself and others. He has compassion for others, and for himself. He does not care for pleasure in any form, unless it be thinking of past sorrows. He relates, not to any anti-hero of Genet, Hemingway, Mailer, Baldwin, Algren, Gide or Dreiser, but to Goethe's Werther. He may be the only modern hero of his "kind" who does not commit suicide in the next-to-last chapter. He is not likeable. He has never loved anyone but his dead dog, Winnie. His affections tend towards the Sky and the Earth. He finds the sky beautiful, the earth dirty. He does everything, but Reluctantly, which one suspects makes him feel like the Knights of Old. "Perhaps my guilt is a wayward apology for living in a world for which I dont feel responsible." He is as sorry, sorry, sorry about his brave, courageous or feeling deeds as if he had himself led all these grown-up children on their abortive crusade knowing full well at the start that it was merely an activity. His mean deeds are similarly Knightly and pragmatic: how many Christians are not a little proud, authorized Baltimore catechism to the contrary, of being malicious to sinners? Christians no longer believe in stamping out what they consider evil, lest they come to resemble Hitler, but they don't mind driving a few nails into it. They have an infinite sympathy for their anguish that the world is not as they were told it should be in childhood, and Rechy's hero is one of these who, despairing, will never become a mess because they are too ungenerous, too cheated of their expectations, and who, victims of bad luck or obtuseness, will never be truly rebellious because they are too spoiled and too self-protective.

This is one of the best first novels in recent years, and Rechy's is a brilliant portrait of this man. Nowhere in the four hundred and ten pages does Rechy lose control of the man he is writing. He never loses his sense of the memoir-character of good first-person-singular novels; where the narrator is sentimental, naïve or downright stupid, and he is very often one or all of the three, one does not find Rechy in the wings signalling to him, he lets him have the stage completely and he is never embarrassed by his hero.

(I should digress here to mention that, contrary to certain other critics of this novel, I do not assume that Rechy is the narrator. Fiction I take it is fiction, and no one will ever convince me that Albertine was Proust's chauffeur.)

Like most picaresque novels, there is a good deal of the travelogue in *City of Night* and Rechy, as his non-fiction pieces on El Paso and Los Angeles indicate, is a master at getting the distinctive and odd quality of a city or a quarter or a milieu into his prose. And he gets it in an attractive, breathy, almost sloppy prose which has the immediacy, fun and discomfort of seeing America by Greyhound bus. This does not always turn to his advantage in other parts of the novel, where his ear finds rather excessive displays of verbiage for rather unremarkable sentiments, as indicated in the first paragraph of this review. But the very good thing about the book, as one compares it in one's mind to so much recent fiction, is that it is not presented and it is not conceived, it is *written*. Rechy is not a great writer (yet?), but he is writing, and he is writing his own book.

City of Night does not have a plot, *per se*. It is a quest novel. Its vicissitudes are those of a very minor Arthurian search, and, while Hell is mentioned often and seriously in the theological sense, it is no paradigm of Dante. It would be boring if it were, most likely, since that aspect of the Joycean-Eliotean idea, though ignored by many a contemporary pseudo-allegorist, has been pretty much exhausted by Harvard and Yale students. (Lord! spare us from any more Fisher kings!) It is instead a naturalistic novel, owing a little, I hope, to the implacable commonness of Horace McCoy and the gatheringness of Whitman. Some of the best parts (especially the Mardi Gras section) seem to show an original interpretation of what Rimbaud, no less, was doing in the "parade" poems and in *A Season in Hell,* without getting into that boring avant-garde version of the French prose poem which is so ubiquitous, or was until two years ago. What comes out in the Mardi Gras section of the book is that atrocious fanfare which Rimbaud celebrated; it is to my mind the finest and most compelling prose realization of derangement through social confrontation in American letters (or English) since *Day of the Locust.* They each have a strength of viewpoint in placing the individual in conflict with, and as victim of, the occasion of a society's self-exorcism which is unequalled since Hawthorne. Rechy's prose is at its best in this New Orleans section of the book. Its repetitions are effective, its insistence persuasive.

In any quest novel, let alone an unanswered-quest novel, the narrative is going to have its ups and downs of interest, and *City of Night* certainly has its ups and downs. For one thing, the quest is too easily exposed, and too early guessed. Secondly, the opposition of Love and Salvation is facile, unless one was brought up a Roman Catholic, a Mormon, or a Jew. Well, the hero was and so was I. But the hero's imposition of destiny in place of a god he will not face is not poignant, though it is naturalistic. The great stroke of the naturalist novelists was that the reader knows more about the character than the character himself does. This Rechy accomplishes. What mars it often is an over writing which makes one feel with some nervousness and loss of faith that Rechy is aiming not at naturalism, but at existentialism. These are the unfortunate passages of the book. And there are others. They are the passages where neither Rechy nor the hero is sure that anyone gets the Point. We excuse this narrative lapse in many a minor novel, knowing full well that the author is laying out the map with too many pins, but in a novel like *City of Night* it is inexcusable. At its worst, it makes one wonder who the hell the author thinks his audience is. Helen Hokinson? Take for example on page 182:

> I needed hungrily to be wanted — but when someone tried to get too close — someone met in the daily excursion through moviehouse balconies, bars, the park — I immediately moved away from him. I seldom saw the same person more than a few times during those months.

If you were awake while reading that's not exactly news. Nor does one feel that it's a sudden moment of self-awareness on the part of the narrator. Not if one has read on page 39:

> With that silver-haired man just now, I had realized this: It would not be in one apartment, with one person, that I would explore the world which had brought me to the city.
> The streets . . . the movie theatres . . . the parks . . . the many, many different rooms: That was the world I would live in.

Well, okay. At that it is preferable to the customary terse understatement which is usually Raymond Chandler masquerading as *The Sun Also Rises.* In writing this, as well as in reading several of the more vicious reviews *City of Night* has received, I cannot but be convinced that Rechy not only has his own voice, but also that it has an almost hypnotic effect on many other writers, which is able to bring out all sorts of bitchy and flatulent attitudes which are otherwise cleverly hidden in conditioned, or assumed, stylistics. (He even manages to get Alfred Chester down to the "Oh, Mary" level.) That's not to say that *any* stylistic power is a good thing, but it's a leg over. And so far he has been entirely superior to his detractors in print. Superior even in tone, I might add, which is something he does not aim at in his book and which they depend on very heavily for effect.

William Carlos Williams has said, "The objective in writing is, to reveal. It is not to teach, not to advertise, not to sell, not even to communicate (for that needs two) but to reveal, which needs no other than the man himself . . . Reveal what? That which is inside the man." I don't think that Rechy has gotten as close to this objective as have Burroughs in *Naked Lunch* and LeRoi Jones in *The System of Dante's Hell,* but neither has anyone else gotten as close as he, in the recent books I've read (prose). It's a funny position to be in, to any degree, because revelation appeals to the artist and to the mass (as those fluky best-seller lists indicate), while the broad-minded, well-informed and -read, critically-well-equipped (notice how many "well"s we have accumulated?), socially *formative* intellectual and literary minds are deeply distrustful. I don't suppose they have trusted anything since the crash of 1929, or at the very latest the Hitler-Stalin pact, compounded by the disclosure of Gide's "white" marriage. (A case in point is Diana Trilling's piece on Allen Ginsberg's reading at Columbia.) Rechy is not in their area of literature, he is out of the woods of professionalism, and from that point of view his book is impervious to the *Partisan Review* type criticism which damns it for being inferior to Dostoevsky and Goethe (both, apparently, thought of as masters of the "well-made" novel!) as well as to the trade journalism of Norman Mailer and Dwight MacDonald. The separation between life and literature will never be established like a Berlin Wall no matter how assertive the critic, it will always drift back and forth according to the temperament of the artist and the temper of the time, creating its endless alienations and difficulties for the writer. In accepting the immediacies of this problem, Rechy has made many obvious difficulties for himself, but what he has lacked in shrewdness is more than compensated for in valor. The hero is a hustler, but the author is not.

[*Kulchur* III:12, Winter 1963]

COMEDY OF MANNERS (AMERICAN)

I guess I am using both "comedy" and "manners" in their loosest application, but my ten best *today* in this category are:

Trouble in Paradise: The greatest drawing-room comedy ever made, it is no surprise that Ernst Lubitsch was the director able to make it that. It has probably the most droll dialogue ever written for a film (in English) and never has Kay Francis been more beautiful, Herbert Marshall more persuasive or Miriam Hopkins cuter. Since manners are the means by which society robs the individual of his sincerity, the plot, as with most other first-rate comedies of manners, involves jewel thieves.

Desire: Another jewel-thief opus, and again by Lubitsch. This time Marlene Dietrich is the beautiful perpetrator and Gary Cooper the gauche American who makes her Love's Victim. It's a brilliantly sly spoof of the switcheroo: be moral and you'll automatically get unhappy; be honest and your gang will turn on you. Again Dietrich has never been *more* beautiful, though the way she is beautiful in *Blonde Venus* and *Shanghai Express* is perhaps more epoch-making.

The Thin Man Series: Every one of these is a joy, wittily written, expertly directed, funny, unassuming, sophisticated. The serious pleasure in them, as in *Trouble in Paradise,* is the playing of the principals. In this genre, no two actors have played more subtly and enchantingly together than Myrna Loy and William Powell. The lines are handled like some spare, dry music, and every raised eyebrow and twitch of the mouth is a delight. And they really seem to *like* each other. For the period, the series is a sort of subliminal ode to the New Deal. Debonair Franklin D is the all-wise leader of the Search, while Eleanor bumbles onto the most important clue and Falla guards the martinis.

The Princess Comes Across: Carole Lombard, the prettiest and best comedienne American films have produced in her charming takeoff of royalty, the manners of High Society — the contrasting Plain Joe of Fred MacMurray, as compared to the way Gary Cooper for one handled this sort of thing and Henry Fonda for another, is so uncharming, though, that it doesn't give Lombard much help. But in

My Man Godfrey: She is just as great, and gets plenty of help from

William Powell and Gail Patrick. This time the rich get it, or at least the
mean rich do, and the manners of the Bum and the Butler are revealed as
preferable to those learned at finishing school. It's interesting that a very
serious social idealism could underlie the crazily funny comedies produced
during the New Deal without either spoiling the fun or degenerating into
caricature. Perhaps having a political ideal was so cheering that one could
permit oneself comedy — at any rate, there have been no good comedies
of this type since, in American films.

Bombshell: Hollywood explores its own manners and discovers they are
supercolossal manifestations of a Heart of Gold. A great Hollywood star
playing a great Hollywood star, Jean Harlow proves, if anyone had any
doubt, that she really was a great star: she can sleep, walk, wiggle, pout,
scream, ride horses, put on *her own* make-up, and toward the end deliver
a long Racinian tirade in classical comic style which is far more impressive
than the famous one in *The Eagle Has Two Heads.* Boy, is she wonderful!
no wonder, etc.

Seven Sinners: Not knowing what else to do with her, one day Universal
sent Dietrich down to the South Seas to investigate the manners of Amer-
ican expatriate "Rock Pool" society, and she discovers a number of good-
hearted lugs going soft in the tropics. The funny version of her earlier
Morocco, this too is about how a girl gets along when she's On Her Own,
with no one to protect her from the snobs but Broderick Crawford, Mischa
Auer and Billy Gilbert, each attacking their characterization à la Restoration
Comedy. The "happy" ending consists only in Dietrich's moral victory: she
gives up dull John Wayne for his own good, thus providing for herself a
future which presumably will be as glamourous as her past.

Flame of New Orleans: Dietrich again, in a period satire on Old Southern
Customs directed by René Clair. She plays dual roles *and* the harpsicord,
and is sought by the oddest rivals for a hand in movies: Bruce Cabot and
Roland Young, who are in love, respectively, with the good-hearted loose-
living River-Scum M. D., and the Gold-digging Parisienne of ancient line-
age. Mischa Auer almost tells Roland Young about her past, but Dietrich
faints. While it is no *Le Million,* Clair encourages her to mock her own
sexual aura, and Dietrich's scenes with Roland Young have a marvelously
confused humor, perfectly placed in the easy, down-by-the-levee pace of
the film.

He Stayed for Breakfast: Loretta Young at *her* most beautiful shows you how to act if a Bolshevik breaks into your Paris apartment and stays, while your fabulously wealthy (and fat − Eugene Pallette) husband is out of town. By the 40s Hollywood was imagining a pampered, gorgeous America charming away the Communist "menace from within," already. But all things being equal, as they had become in the birth of Hollywood uncertainty, it seemed safer to have it all take place in Paris and if there were to be a menace it seemed nicer to have an astute comedian, Melvyn Douglas, do the harmless menacing. Besides, if your strongest relation to Capitalism is Eugene Pallette, it better all happen in France. Very funny dialogue and situation presents a frequently encountered crisis in the comedy of manners of all periods: the milieu is miraculously elegant and articulate, but the articulation forces the heroine to kick over the traces if she is to end up human and justify the film. In this case Loretta Young shoots off the tip of her husband's pinkie and elopes with the Bolshevik − not to Russia, not to Outer Mongolia, not even to Albania: home to America! where presumably the difference in their mores will be welded together in a factory in Detroit. Brilliantly played under Alexander Hall's direction, the very lack of social content seems to have made every one concerned whip up this undecided political satire to a giddy pitch. Accidentally, Eugene Pallette is allowed to create a characterization of a Capitalist which should still warm the hearts of Communists everywhere. It's a really pertinent movie, but behind the adroitness of its delivery is a rather brutal fact: the boom was being lowered on all comedies of manners which had any pertinence socially whatsoever. This film, like *Ninotchka*, is the "I kissed thee 'ere I killed thee" of Hollywood to Communism -- an attempt to deal with an issue which was too great for a *hobbled* public medium to deal with, and unfortunately Hollywood gave over to a sniveling desire for status in a society which didn't know what it was doing anyway. It was not that there were Communists in Hollywood that fouled things up, but that there was weak-minded greed and too many near-shots. Hercules knew enough *not* to let go of the snake's neck. The movie is wonderful, because having its own personality it is stand-alone on the brink of this tragedy.

Ninotchka: A very funny thing happened to MGM with *Ninotchka*. Ernst Lubitsch, never known for his interest in political issues in his movies, turned this political satire into a superb comedy of manners. Where the script indicates that the film is *about* the rehabilitation of

an hitherto unattractive Communist woman on her first trip outside the
USSR by a Romantic Capitalist, Lubitsch turns it, aided by casting, into
a comedy about whether two charming people from totally different
backgrounds can communicate closely enough to fall in love. Casting
Garbo as the Commissar settled the issue in the first reel: the greatest
star in film history arrives in Paris in a 'communist' get-up which looked
remarkably like what she appeared (and appears) in on the streets of
New York and in the newspapers. Everything Melvyn Douglas as the
lover, or Adrian as the designer, did thereafter to transform this chrysalis
into a butterfly was sheer fun. Absolutely no political content exists in
this film, which is the sign of its integrity, since none was felt. Despite the
vague ideological framework, if Garbo had not returned to Paris at the
end Melvyn Douglas, spokesman of Capitalism, would have been a fool
not to have joined her in Moscow or Leningrad, and the whole audience
knew it. Apart from its excellence as an urbane confrontation in a hum-
orous way of two different kinds of ways of living, it's amazing that
Louis B. Mayer let Lubitsch get away with it in the era of Andy Hardy.
Garbo is, as always, the end. Every actress on stage or screen should
study her voice.

       And it's a terrible thing that I can't tell you how great
Woman Chases Man, Miriam Hopkins and Joel McCrea, continues to be,
which was made in a more dramatic, and thus personal, period, when
you disliked accents because they were affected, and you disliked the
rich because you wanted their money, and sexual attraction took its
true place in the firmament of "ideas." But that would be the 11th
Great Flick.

[*Kulchur* II:5, Spring 1962]

LARRY RIVERS: A MEMOIR

I first met Larry Rivers in 1950. When I started coming down to New York from Harvard, Larry was in Europe, and friends had said we would like each other. Finally, at for me a very literary cocktail party at John Ashbery's we did meet, and we did like each other: I thought he was crazy and he thought I was even crazier. I was very shy, which he thought was intelligence; he was garrulous, which I assumed was brilliance — and on such misinterpretations, thank heavens, many a friendship is based. On the other hand, perhaps it was not a misinterpretation: certain of my literary "heroes" of the *Partisan Review* variety present at that party paled in significance when I met Larry, and through these years have remained pale while Larry has been something of a hero to me, which would seem to make me intelligent and Larry brilliant. Who knows?

The milieu of those days, and it's funny to think of them in such a way since they are so recent, seems odd now. We were all in our early twenties. John Ashbery, Barbara Guest, Kenneth Koch and I, being poets, divided our time between the literary bar, the San Remo, and the artists' bar, the Cedar Tavern. In the San Remo we argued and gossiped; in the Cedar we often wrote poems while listening to the painters argue and gossip. So far as I know nobody painted in the San Remo while they listened to the writers argue. An interesting sidelight to these social activities was that for most of us non-academic, and indeed non-literary poets in the sense of the American scene at the time, the painters were the only generous audience for our poetry, and most of us read first publicly in art galleries or at The Club. The literary establishment cared about as much for our work as the Frick cared for Pollock and de Kooning, not that we cared any more for establishments than they did, all of the disinterested parties being honorable men.

Then there was great respect for anyone who did anything marvelous: when Larry introduced me to de Kooning I nearly got sick, as I almost did when I met Auden; if Jackson Pollock tore the door off the men's room in the Cedar it was something he just did and was interesting, not an annoyance. You couldn't see into it anyway, and besides there was then a sense of genius. Or what Kline used to call "the dream." Newman was at that time considered a temporarily silent oracle, being ill, Ad Reinhardt the most shrewd critic of the emergent "art world," Meyer Schapiro a god and Alfred Barr right up there alongside him but more distant, Holger Cahill another god but one who had abdicated to become more interested in "the thing we're doing," Clement Greenberg the discoverer, Harold Rosenberg the analyzer, and so on and so on. Tom Hess had written the important book. Elaine de Kooning was the White Goddess: she knew everything, told little of it though she talked a lot, and we all adored (and adore) her. She is graceful.

Into this scene Larry came rather like a demented telephone. Nobody knew whether they wanted it in the library, the kitchen or the toilet, but it was electric. Nor did he. The single most important event in his artistic career was when de Kooning said his painting was like pressing your face into wet grass. From the whole jazz scene, which had gradually diminished to a mere recreation, Larry had emerged into the world of art with the sanction of one of his own gods, and indeed the only living one.

It is interesting to think of 1950-52, and the styles of a whole group of young artists whom I knew rather intimately. It was a liberal education on top of an academic one. Larry was chiefly involved with Bonnard and Renoir at first, later Manet and Soutine. Joan Mitchell — Duchamp; Mike Goldberg — Cézanne-Villon-de Kooning; Helen Frankenthaler — Pollock-Miró; Al Leslie — Motherwell; De Niro — Matisse; Nell Blaine — Helion; Hartigan — Pollock-Guston; Harry Jackson — a lot of Matisse with a little German expressionism; Jane Freilicher — a more subtle combination of Soutine with some Monticelli and Moreau appearing through the paint. The impact of THE NEW AMERICAN PAINTING on this group was being avoided rather self-consciously rather than exploited. If you live in the studio next to Brancusi, you try to think about Poussin. If you drink with Kline you tend to do your black-and-whites in pencil on paper. The artists I knew at that time knew perfectly well who was Great and they weren't going to begin to imitate their works, only their spirit. When someone did a false Clyfford Still or Rothko, it was talked about for weeks. They hadn't read Sartre's *Being and Nothingness* for nothing.

Larry was especially interested in the vast range of possibilities of art. Perhaps because of his experience as a jazz musician, where everything can become fixed so quickly in style, become "the sound," he has moved restlessly from phase to phase. Larry always wanted to see something when he painted, unlike the then-prevalent conceptualized approach. No matter what stylistic period he was in, the friends he spent most time with were invariably subjects in some sense, more or less recognizable, and of course his two sons and his mother-in-law who lived with him were the most frequent subjects (he was separated from his wife, Augusta). His mother-

in-law, Mrs. Bertha Burger, was the most frequent subject. She was called
Berdie by everyone, a woman of infinite patience and sweetness, who
held together a Bohemian household of such staggering complexity it
would have driven a less great woman mad. She had a natural grace of
temperament which overcame all obstacles and irritations. (During her
fatal illness she confessed to me that she had once actually disliked two
of Larry's friends because they had been "mean" to her grandsons, and
this apologetically!) She appears in every period: early Soutinesque
painting with a cat; at an impressionistic breakfast table; in the semi-
abstract paintings of her seated in a wicker chair; as the double nude,
very realistic, now in the collection of the Whitney Museum; in the later
The Athlete's Dream, which she especially enjoyed because I posed with
her and it made her less self-conscious if she was in a painting with a
friend; she is also all the figures in the Museum of Modern Art's great
painting *The Pool.* Her gentle interestedness extended beyond her own
family to everyone who frequented the house, in a completely incurious
way. Surrounded by painters and poets suddenly in mid-life, she had an
admirable directness with esthetic decisions: "it must be very good work,
he's such a wonderful person." Considering the polemics of the time,
this was not only a relaxing attitude, it was an adorable one. For many
of us her death was as much the personal end of a period as Pollock's
death was that of a public one.

I mention these details of Rivers' life because, in the sense that
Picasso meant it, his work is very much a diary of his experience. He is in-
spired directly by visual stimulation and his work is ambitious to save
these experiences. Where much of the art of our time has been involved
with direct conceptual or ethical considerations, Rivers has chosen to
mirror his preoccupations and enthusiasms in an unprogrammatic way.
As an example, I think that he personally was very awed by Rothko and
that this reveals itself in the seated figures of 1953-54; at the same time I
know that a rereading of *War and Peace,* and his idea of Tolstoy's life,
prompted him to commence work on *Washington Crossing the Delaware,*
a non-historical, non-philosophical work, the impulse for which I at first
thought was hopelessly corny until I saw the painting finished. Rivers
veers sharply, as if totally dependent on life impulses, until one observes
an obsessively willful insistence on precisely what he is interested in. This
goes for the father of our country as well as for the later Camel and
Tareyton packs. Who, he seems to be saying, says they're corny? This is
the opposite of pop art. He is never naive and never oversophisticated.

Less known than his jazz interests are Larry's literary ones. He has kept, sporadically, a fairly voluminous and definitely scandalous journal, has written some good poems of a diaristic (boosted by surrealism) nature, and collaborated with several poets (including myself) who have posed for him, mainly I think to keep them quiet while posing and to relax himself when not painting or sculpting. The literary side of his activity has resulted mainly in the poem-paintings with Kenneth Koch, a series of lithographs [*Stones*] with me, and our great collaborative play *Kenneth Koch, a Tragedy,* which cannot be printed because it is so filled with 50s art gossip that everyone would sue us. This latter work kept me amused enough to continue to pose for the big nude which took so many months to finish. That is one of Larry's strategies to keep you coming back to his studio, or was when he couldn't afford a professional model. The separation of the arts, in the "pure" sense, has never interested him. As early as 1952, when John Myers and Herbert Machiz were producing the New York Artists' Theatre, Larry did a set for a play of mine, *Try! Try!* At the first run-through I realized it was all wrong and withdrew it. He, however, insisted that if he had done the work for the set I should be willing to rewrite to my own satisfaction, and so I rewrote the play for Anne Meacham, J.D. Cannon, Louis Edmonds and Larry's set, and that is the version printed by Grove Press. Few people are so generous toward the work of others.

As I said earlier, Larry is restless, impulsive and compulsive. He loves to work. I remember a typical moment in the late 50s when both Joan Mitchell and I were visiting the Hamptons and we were all lying on the beach, a state of relaxation Larry can never tolerate for long. Joan was wearing a particularly attractive boating hat and Larry insisted that they go back to his studio so he could make a drawing of her. It is a beautiful drawing, an interesting moment in their lives, and Joan was not only pleased to be drawn, she was relieved because she is terribly vulnerable to sunburn. As Kenneth Koch once said of him, "Larry has a floating subconscious — he's all intuition and no sense."

That's an interesting observation about the person, but actually Larry Rivers brings such a barrage of technical gifts to each intuitive occasion that the moment is totally transformed. Many of these gifts were acquired in the same manner as his talents in music and literature, through practice. Having been hired by Herbie Fields' band in his teens he became adept at the saxophone, meeting a group of poets who interested him he absorbed, pro or con, lots of ideas about style in poetry, and attending classes at Hans Hofmann's school plunged him into activities which were to make him one of the best draftsmen in contemporary art and one of the most subtle and particular colorists. This has been accomplished through work rather than intellection. And here an analogy to jazz can be justified: his hundreds of drawings are each like a separate performance, with its own occasion and subject, and what has been "learned" from the performance is not just the technical facility of the classical pianists' octaves or the studies in a *Grande Chaumière* class, but the ability to deal with the increased skills that deepening of subject matter and the risks of anxiety-dictated variety demand for clear expression. When Rivers draws a nose, it is my nose, your nose, his nose, Gogol's nose, and the nose from a drawing instruction manual, and it is the result of highly conscious skill.

There is a little bit of Hemingway in his attitude toward ability, toward what you do to a canvas or an armature. His early painting, *The Burial,* is really, in a less arrogant manner than Hemingway's, "getting into the ring" with Courbet (*The Funeral at Ornans*), just as his nude portrait of me started in his mind from envy of the then newly acquired Géricault slave with the rope at the Metropolitan Museum, the portrait *Augusta* from a Delacroix; and even this year he is still fighting it out, this time with David's *Napoleon.* As with his friends, as with cigarette and cigar boxes, maps, and animals, he is always engaged in an esthetic athleticism which sharpens the eye, hand and arm in order to beat the bugaboos of banality and boredom, deliberately invited into the painting and then triumphed over.

What his work has always had to say to me, I guess, is to be more keenly interested while I'm still alive. And perhaps this is the most important thing art can say.

[From the catalog of the Larry Rivers retrospective exhibition, Poses Institute of Fine Arts, Brandeis University, 1965]

THE GRAND MANNER OF MOTHERWELL

When a major artist has a major retrospective and he is an American and
it is in an American museum — as in this instance of Robert Motherwell
now at New York's Museum of Modern Art — all sorts of harrowing ex-
citements occur which involve all concerned. For the artist it is the tem-
porary summation of his achievement thus far, an exposure which no sen-
sible person should want and many artists don't want. Who would demand
it of the other arts — the more or less full range of sensibility in two hours
of attention, let's say, from a composer, a poet, a novelist, an actor or
playwright, a great diva? Each has a relatively vast temporal area to prove
and reprove, correct or reassert the grandeur of the vision. But painters
and sculptors are expected to be able to affirm, by the simple method of
collection and installation, the verity and importance of their preoccupa-
tions, instantaneously and simultaneously.

This is right, ultimately, because their arts do not use time as a duration;
they use it as conception. We love the "long time" look of Rembrandt and
Vermeer as we love the languorous ease of a cabaletta in Bellini or Verdi,
and we love the quickness of the whiplashes and drastic lines of Pollock
and Motherwell as we love the speed of transition of motive and musical
thought in Stravinsky and Webern. But these are not identifications, they
are correspondences. In painting and sculpture we perceive fast or slow
time as a frontal onslaught, not a cumulative experience.

Robert Motherwell's work is a frontal experience par excellence. His in-
sistence has been on the painting as "wall" — flat surface, two dimensional,
no illusionism. Whether measured five by ten inches or eight by twenty
feet, his work, like that of Franz Kline, is concerned with a frontal assault
on the view of significant two-dimensional forms. Where much twentieth-
century art naively assumes that to *project* another dimension is something
extraordinary, here we find the clarification of means between painting
and sculpture, the extreme decision on which properties belong to which.
Beside this, op art becomes merely *trompe l'oeil*, the old fakir's trick,
about as convincing as Dali's recent conception of the discovery of America.
(What has come out of *trompe l'oeil*, for example, the early Dali in one
way and Joseph Cornell's wonderful work in another, is of course some-
thing else.) But in every way the great truth must begin with the simple
truth: that painting is made with paint and canvas, that poetry is made with
words. The irritating thing about Philistine criticism is that sometimes it's

right: some assemblagists can not draw: some pop artists can only render what someone else has designed. There's nothing wrong with this as long as the result is a work of art, but it does not ensure a long career of delight, but rather one of repetition of what one can do. (This goes for several expert realists as well — how many melancholy ladies do you want to see having the eternal breakfast? And now that photography has zoomed in, how many repetitious forms of your least favourite actress, or even most favourite, do you want to contemplate?)

But to get back to the harrowing aspect of a retrospective in another sense, the curator's, my own: nobody who hasn't done a selection has any idea of how anxiety-making it is. You make your preferences known to the artist, and in this case a very grand, generous, open-minded one. He says he is satisfied, or more so, with the works you are including. And immediately your mind is flooded with mentions by critics of other works which are superlatively important to the representation. And you think of the walls. You think of the walls here and in Europe and what they can show and what you must *not* put in for the sake of the other works, and of the exact painting you have decided to exclude because you think another is more important — and then you have the appalling realization that the thought-word you used was "think"! Help! Are you sure? With a major artist it is very difficult to be sure between two important paintings, and suddenly you wish you were doing a show of the Pont Aven school or the Barbizons or the surrealists, because to no single artist would you be responsible if someone wouldn't lend a key work, or if your judgment went astray. But one-man shows are what you want to see, what you want to do, and this is the artist you want to present: so you jump, knowing full well that in Europe retrospectives of living artists abound, but here until very recently they were very rare, and that you have put your head in the noose of your admiration for this artist, and if the show doesn't say what you want it to say, it is nobody's fault but your own.

Motherwell is tough, sassy, and, yes, elegant, as a painter. Where a noble motif appears, as in the first *Spanish Elegies*, he will pursue it and nag it for fifteen years, proving that tragedy, disillusion, and diffidence are our daily inevitable fare, and thus producing some of the great paintings by an American. Similarly with the collages: his imitators get the glamour, but they miss the physical tearingness and destruction beyond technical need, the sparseness and cynicism which is more powerful than mere simplicity. He always seems to be wryly reflecting that to do less is more, and getting no satisfaction from the thought. What is difficult in Motherwell's work is not the rationale for its surface attraction, but the interconnection of the individual works.

What he is making, with all its variety, is THE WORK, as Mallarmé intended, however various the poems, to be writing THE BOOK. Among the contemporary Americans he relates, oddly enough, most closely to de Kooning: in their utterly different personalities one finds a strong central impulse which can not confine itself to one style or language, to any one mode of communication, so proud and anxious are their desires. They are probably both flirting with the Absolute, and if they are, she keeps turning a different shoulder to them, or telling them to make a slight adjustment of the drawing of that shoulder they drew the day before last.

I first met Motherwell in East Hampton in, probably, 1952. When we did talk later, it was almost always about poetry: Apollinaire, Baudelaire, Jacob, Reverdy, Rilke (not so much), and Lorca (lots), and we also got to Wallace Stevens and William Carlos Williams. I had been tremendously impressed by the Documents of Modern Art Series which Motherwell had edited (indeed, it was The Gospels for myself and many other poets). At that time we never discussed painting, so far as I remember.

He paints, makes collages, draws (this year he made six hundred small inks on Japan paper in six weeks!), teaches, lectures, travels, and also serves on certain committees in which he feels the contemporary artist should be involved, or at least acknowledged. Motherwell outside the studio is an engaging, wily conversationalist. He is not gregarious, but he is socially expansive and curious. He is very attentive to what you have to say, and will not hesitate to point out, quietly but definitely, where he finds your thinking going wrong. If he finds you thinking right, or if you have a really fresh idea, he acts as if you had just given him a present he'd been longing for. He is open-minded and sharply critical: he was the first abstract expressionist to say pop art was "okay," and the first to admit publicly that he didn't like it although he felt it had a youthful joy which would doubtless lead certain individual artists onward. This latter quality is something few if any professional art critics have noted, so eager have they been to tie pop art to a social millstone and dump it in the Hudson.

Motherwell is fifty this year, looks younger, and is definitely interested in Onward. Contrary to what some critics have said, particularly in the daily and weekly papers, pop and op art have not at all "killed" other contemporary movements, least of all abstract expressionism, as evidenced by the two excellent exhibitions of the New York School given recently at the University of Pennsylvania and the Los Angeles County Museum.

As a matter of fact, pop and op have tended to stimulate a way of looking, particularly at the abstract expressionists and hard-edge painters, which reveals new qualities in their works. Ellsworth Kelly, for example, is more interesting rather than less if you have just come from a show of Anusz-kiewicz or Poons, and you see more in a Motherwell rather than less if you have just been studying a Rosenquist or a Dine.

Variety is what, of course, abstract expressionism has insisted on all along, and its originators have offered it to us consistently: there has been no "school" in the history of art that I know of which has included artists so totally different in style and subject matter as Pollock, de Kooning, Rothko, Newman, Kline, Gottlieb, Motherwell, and others. (A variety, incidentally, which pop and op art adherents have a hard time maintaining among their members.) Motherwell's own development from the early forties has included a great many changes in style and confrontation. There is a characteristic Motherwell touch, placement, and attack, but the uses to which they are put from period to period are enormously different.

Modern beauty is what interests him. Modern beauty excites first and interests afterward. The art of other periods interests first and then gradually becomes exciting by its beauty.

Motherwell's work continually fluctuates between chance and deliberation. New motifs arise from visual and subconscious experiences (the *Summertime in Italy* and the *Beside the Sea* series, for example, were inspired visually; the *Lyric Suite* series and the *Automatisms* subconsciously), yet the *Elegies to the Spanish Republic* continue obsessively through every period since their inception in 1948, as do certain aspects of the collages and his almost hedonistic delight in the textures, qualities, and colors of Paper, which in Motherwell's oeuvre must have a capital P, whether one speaks of collage, watercolor and ink, or lithographic media. A piece of paper can inspire him as much as a Civil War.

The other capital P in his work is Poetry. Without being literary in content, his work continually reflects the importance of poetry in his life and art. One of his great early collages is titled *The Poet*, as is one of his most recent lithographs (the latter is the mirror image of the shape of a P).

The *Elegy to the Spanish Republic* motif was discovered while making a drawing for a poem by Harold Rosenberg, and its first major development was titled *At Five in the Afternoon* (1949), the repeated refrain of Garcia Lorca's great elegy for the bullfighter Ignacio Sánchez Mejías, a poem which undoubtedly suggested the title for the whole series. Such other titles as *Mallarmé's Swan* and *Throw of the Dice, The Voyage* and

The Joy of Living, Jour la Maison, Nuit la Rue, and *Automatisms* indicate
his homage to Mallarmé, Baudelaire, and the surrealist poets of France, re-
spectively,

One should also add Wallace Stevens to this roster of enthusiasms, as
the American poet probably most similar in sensibility to Motherwell.
Stevens's "Thirteen Ways of Looking at a Blackbird" is almost a paradigm
of Motherwell's conception of the "series," in which variations on a visual
motif invite the artist and the viewer to see things with as much ingenuity
and insight available to each without violating the essential identity of the
initial image.

In this way, Motherwell brings the variation idea into the area of por-
traiture, in his case a series of portraits which reveals aspects of a given im-
age rather than a face or a torso, or a ballerina backstage, as in Degas.
Motherwell is every bit as enamoured of the rough triangle and the slightly
irregular circle as Degas was of the backstage theatre and the racetrack. As
Franz Kline once said: "It's a wonderful thing to be in love with the
square."

Only a truly intracontinental artist (Washington, California, New York,
Massachusetts, Oregon, Mexico, Canada, East Hampton, Cape Cod) could
dash into European culture with such zest and alacrity as Motherwell did,
while retaining his identity as an American, admiring, inspired, but not at
all swamped by it all, as were most American artists in the past.

Short of a national disaster, there could never be a question of Mother-
well becoming an expatriate, perhaps because he believes that, after
Picasso, Mattisse, and Miró, modernity in art lives here.

Motherwell is very conscious of distinctions and, for all the spontaneity
in his work, of what must be done for and about art right now in an his-
torical sense. Recently on a Channel 13 television program, Bryon Robert-
son, director of the Whitechapel Gallery in London, asked him if he
"could make some absolutely final and ultimate and all-embracing state-
ment" about his work as a whole. Motherwell replied:

Being able to talk about only one thing during two minutes or so, I
would choose to talk about the ethical character of art which, I think,
moves us even more than art's delight in sensuality, or its beauty of for-
mal structure. I am not talking about painting with a moral, like Aesop's
Fables, of course: moralisms belong to the lowest forms of painting —
genre painting, propaganda, popular religious art, advertising, Madison
Avenue.

What I mean by an artist's ethic is what he insists on having in a picture, and what, equally strongly, he can not allow, through conviction.

In my case, I allow no nostalgia, no sentimentalism, no propaganda, no 'spelling out,' no autobiography, no violation of the nature of the canvas, no clichés, no illusionism, no description, no predetermined endings, no seduction, no charm, no relaxation, no mere taste, no obviousness, no coldness . . . .

On the contrary, I insist on immediacy, passion or tenderness, beingness as such, sheer presence, objectivity, true invention and true resolution, light, the unexpected, direct colors (sky blue, grass green, English vermilion, the earth colors: ocher, sienna, and umber, and black and white), and a certain broad masculinity and emotional weight that is hard to describe.

There are my moral acceptances and rejections. Other painters have other values.

But there is nothing mysterious about any artists values *if* one's mind and heart are sympathetic, clear, and unprejudiced, a condition less common than one might suppose.

When this interview was first shown, some of the artists who saw it said, "Oh, yeah," and others said, "Wow!" I myself thought the tone of it quite unlike "the Motherwell I know." But a little later something about it reminded me of all those battles fought by Motherwell and his colleagues — the abstract expressionists — against provincialism and regionalism in American art, for recognition of a new, clear and passionate expression, the panels and forums, the journals, the letters to museums and newspapers demanding a change in our way of feeling a painting, and an acknowledgement of the new vision.

That battle was won and a younger generation — an Andy Warhol or a Larry Poons — has a quick, lively, and responsive audience at hand because of these earlier victories. Motherwell himself could certainly rest secure in his accomplishment. But the modern artist has no recognizable laurels to crown him and no inclination to rest. Like the rest of us, but more as an exemplar than a companion, he has his arrogant insistence on joy and his fateful cognition of the deaths around us. In presenting his exhibition, we are joining Motherwell's passionate affirmation of experience against despair. With each line, mass, and torn edge, he is, like Apelles, erecting for us the noble wall of his aspiration against the darkness without.

[*Vogue,* October 1965]

PREFACE TO ERJE AYDEN'S
THE CRAZY GREEN OF SECOND AVENUE

Erje Ayden is the traditional "foreigner," perhaps no more foreign to our language and ways than was D. H. Lawrence, perhaps as foreign to them as Joseph Conrad was to English at the beginning of his great labors. Like Lawrence he has the advantage of viewing our mores and our verbal locutions from alien and strong tradition; like Conrad he would like to have a *rhetorical* hero of undeniable strength and certitude appear in his writings, but life cannot reveal one. Like so many who refreshed the languages of the world in the 20th century, he is an alien wherever he is, probing and disfiguring ordinary reality with a sense of popularity, and accepting its most peculiar and neurotic aspects as quite unexceptional. Like most writers of power and vivid interest, Ayden is able to transform his miscalculations and misunderstandings into personal expressive advantages. We must admire this unless we are willing to give up William Carlos Williams' dictum that the American language is distinct from the English, and lapse into a long development of Mandarin style which would be indistinguishable from the tiring mistake of the English, of the French, and of the German.

Because of the moral ambivalence of another tradition, Ayden is one of the sexiest writers we have; because of his struggles with acquired language he has a vigor uncommon among our novelists; without the mannerist inclinations of Salinger, Pynchon, Barth, or Updike, he is able to convey the real trouble underneath the bizarre and the banal. In adopting Fitzgerald as a model, Ayden links himself with other off-shoots of that germinal stylist's attitude: Nathaniel West, Horace McCoy and even Dashiel Hammett. He has the same brevity, the same swift pace, the same tendency of observation and impatience with analysis. Neither daring nor caring to make a beautiful English sentence, he is able to get some of that marvelous Fitzgerald quickness and pointedness, which in the latter's case made Hemingway's most machine-gunned sentences seem rather studied. As with Gatsby and Rosemary, Ayden's characters are quickly fixed by events in an airy space which belongs to no one, least of all them. Through Ayden's eyes we see an "Amerika" as odd as Kafka's; as funny as absurdly sad. Nobody thinks that things are as they seem, but Ayden makes the gap between seeming and being considerably wider. Operating in this gap his people (Elliot in *Crazy Green,* "I" in *Confessions of a Nowaday Child,* the hero of *From Hauptbahnhof I Took a Train* who keeps changing his name) are always on the go, whether their destination is set or not, in order to keep alive.

[1965]

PREFACE TO A. B. SPELLMAN'S
THE BEAUTIFUL DAYS

Spellman writes lean, strong, sexy poems. He cuts through a lot of contemporary nonsense to what is actually happening to him, and that actually reveals his real voice sounding above the inspired or the willed (in the moral sense) technical choices. As the French poet Marcellin Pleynet observed, ". . . what speaks in what is happening is thought — the thought of what is happening." Spellman's celebrations of his loves are never without pain, his laments for his dead have a strange practicality — "if i can care for the newly dead as far as from here/ to here/ i may be thought not to be among them." His poems speak about an existence happening between extreme heat and extreme cold, between black and white, fire and snow, and what a poet's sensibility must ask of him. He's honest, so naturally a lot of them are perfect.

[1965]

INTRODUCTION TO EDWIN DENBY'S
DANCERS BUILDINGS AND PEOPLE IN THE STREETS

In "Some Thoughts about Classicism and George Balanchine," Edwin Denby writes that Balanchine's remarks had suggested to him ". . . the idea, too, of style as something a man, who has spent many years of his life working in an art, loves with attentive pertinacity." This idea, I think, is the basis of Denby's prose and poetry, a style which ". . . demands a constant attention to details which the public is not meant to notice, which only professionals spot, so unemphatic do they remain in performance." They were speaking of ballet performance, but the idea is equally true of Denby's writing performance, and one of the important secrets of its pleasures.

Since Edwin Denby is a good friend of mine, there are other secrets I should reveal. He sees and hears more clearly than anyone else I have ever known. No expressive or faulty quiver in a *battement,* no ingenious or clumsy transition in a musical score (whether Drigo or Gunther Schuller), no squiggle in a painting and no adverb, seems ever to escape his attention as to its relevance in the work as a whole. Having a basically generous nature, he is not at all guilty about pointing out mistakes and, unlike many poets who are also critics, he feels the moral necessity to point them out lest his praise be diminished by an atmosphere of professional "kindness." Most fortunately, his lyrical poetic gifts are tempered by the journalist's concern for facts and information. He works very hard at the above-mentioned "style" so as to give us a whole spectum of possibilities: what he saw and heard, what he felt, what he thinks the intention was, what the event seemed to be, what the facts surrounding it were, what the audience responded to, leaving open with a graciousness worthy of Théophile Gautier the ultimate decision of the reader pro or contra his own opinion as critic. Thus, he restores criticism to writing, to *belles lettres* if you wish, to the open dialogue of opinion and discussion between writer and reader which is nonaggressive and has faith in a common interest as the basis of intellectual endeavor. Few critics are so happy as he to receive your re-interpretation or correction of what he has already seen or heard and already written about. He is truly and deeply interested in a civilized, open-minded way.

On the other hand, he will not just put up with anything. Recently, at the première of Balanchine's *Don Quixote,* he was asked what he thought of the new work. Denby said, "Marvelous! I was very moved."

"I was moved right out of the theatre," his interrogator replied.

"That's where you belong, then," Denby said in the gentlest of tones.

He is always there, telling you what he sees and hears and feels and esteems, not caring whether you agree or not, because it is a friendly parlance about matters which are mutually important. The ballet, the theatre, painting and poetry, our life accidentally in co-existence, is a rather large provenance which he tactfully negotiates and notates. As a theatre man he is interested in The Public, and this gives his criticism a broad, general applicability, moral as much as esthetic, for all its special knowledge and expertise. He is interested in his society, and those societies not his, without sentimentality. For our own society, how we act and what we mean, I cannot think that the two *Lectures* ("Forms in Motion" and "Dancers, Buildings") have less than a major pertinence. For other societies Denby's essays have illuminations about us which are not available elsewhere and are admirably understated.

Denby is as attentive to people walking in the streets or leaning against a corner, in any country he happens to be in, as he is to the more formal and exacting occasions of art and the theatre. He brings a wide range of experience to the expression of these insights: his acting and adaptations for the theatre here and in Germany (as John Houseman recently pointed out, he was not only the adaptor but also the rear legs of the horse in Orson Welles' version of Labiche's *Horse Eats Hat*); his work as ballet critic on the *New York Herald Tribune*; his acting in the films of Rudolph Burckhardt and other "underground" film-makers; his more personal and more hermetic involvement with his poems; his constant traveling and inquisitive scholarship; all these activities contribute a wide range of reference for comparison and understanding of intricate occasions, as well as of complicated implications in occasions seemingly obvious and general.

Like Lamb and Hazlitt, he has lightness and deftness of tone, and a sharp, amused intelligence, as evident in the method of perceiving as in the subject matter itself. Much of his prose is involved with the delineation of sensibility in its experience of time: what happens, and how, if at all? what does each second mean, and how is the span of attention used to make it a longer or shorter experience? is Time in itself beautiful,

or is its quality merely decorable or decorous? Somehow, he gives an
equation in which attention equals Life, or is its only evidence, and this
in turn gives each essay, whatever the occasional nature of its subject,
a larger applicability we seldom find elsewhere in contemporary criticism.

[1965]

GREY FOX PRESS PAPERBACKS